he paintings and line drawings not credited are by the author.

he author's illustrations were created with ink, colored pencils, and acrylic paint on 140-lb
otton paper, manila tagboard, and Masonite panels.

ataloging-in-Publication Data has been applied for and may be obtained from the Library of Congress.

BN 978-1-4197-3193-8

xt and illustrations copyright © 2021 S. D. Nelson
dited by Howard W. Reeves
ok design by Heather Kelly

inted and bound in China
9 8 7 6 5 4 3 2

brams Books for Young Readers are available at special discounts when purchased in quantity for premiums and
omotions as well as fundraising or educational use. Special editions can also be created to specification. For details,
ntact specialsales@abramsbooks.com or the address below.

rams® is a registered trademark of Harry N. Abrams, Inc.

ABRAMS The Art of Books
195 Broadway, New York, NY 10007
abramsbooks.com

Fort Laramie, *circa 1840*,
*by Alfred Jacob Miller shows
the fort and a nearby encampment
of visiting Indians.*

CRAZY HO
AND CUST

~ BORN ENEMIE

S. D. Nelson

Abrams Books for Young Readers

New York

For us and them
The different tribes of men
Joined together in the end

Two spirited boys, both alike in worthiness and desire, were bound against each other from birth. Like all boys, they laughed and played. Both loved riding horses and were especially good at it. They thrilled to the pounding of their horses' hooves on the earth and the rush of wind in their hair. The two youths were taught that personal glory could be won through violent conflict. It was this fatal teaching that would form their destiny and bring a dark end. Shaped by their two different warrior cultures, they grew into manhood, only to meet beneath a blue sky on the western prairies of America in an epic fight—the Battle of the Little Bighorn.

Young Crazy Horse and George Armstrong Custer—born enemies

"My voice is for war!"
—GEORGE ARMSTRONG CUSTER, age seven

1839: George Armstrong Custer Is Born in New Rumley, Ohio

Emanuel Henry Custer was a widower with three children. After the death of his first wife, he married a woman who had three children from a previous marriage. It was from this second marriage to Maria Ward Kirkpatrick that young George Armstrong Custer was born. His mother and older sisters doted on him, spoiling him. As the child grew and began to talk, he tried to pronounce his middle name, "Armstrong." To everyone's delight, the word came out as "Autie." Ever after, his family called the blue-eyed boy "Autie." The Custer home provided common comfort. There was always enough food for a growing boy. His father was a blacksmith and a farmer on land that once belonged to Indians. There were always chickens, cows, and horses about. Young Armstrong helped his father in the blacksmith shop and took right to riding the varied horses in the corral. Emanuel's smiles and embraces made it clear that he loved his spirited son. But the prideful man had strong, dark opinions about the ways of this world and voiced them loudly.

Autie and his father

> "Come, Grandson, I want to tell you a hero story."
> —A Lakota Elder

Circa 1840: Crazy Horse Is Born on the Open Prairies of Present-Day South Dakota Near Bear Butte

The Lakota holy man, named Tasunke Witco, raised the boy in his lodge. The child was different. He did not have bronze-colored skin and raven-black hair like the other children of his tribe. He was born of mixed blood—part Lakota and part white. The Lakota historian Joseph Marshall says they called him "Light Hair" because of his "light brown hair and fair complexion." Tasunke Witco had many wives. (Having more than one wife was a common practice among the Lakota people.) No one knows for certain the identity of Light Hair's biological father. He may have been a French-American fur trader. One of Tasunke Witco's wives, Rattling Blanket Woman, was Light Hair's birth mother. In a state of depression, she hanged herself when Light Hair was only four years old. Thereafter, the boy was cared for by the other wives and older sister of the family. The old ones said, "A boy will learn the way of the warrior from his fathers and grandfathers after he learns courage from his mothers and grandmothers." Light Hair did not smile often and stayed distant from others.

Light Hair with his mother

3

> "When I was merging upon manhood, my every thought
> was ambitious—not to be wealthy, not to be learned, but to be great."
> —GEORGE ARMSTRONG CUSTER

A Born Soldier

Even though the Custer family lived in the northern state of Ohio, Emanuel supported the racist ideas shared by many white people living in the southern slave states. They insisted that people with black-colored skin were subhuman and should be used like farm animals. Autie's father also had little regard for Indians and Mexicans, whom he thought to be inferior half-wits. Emanuel belonged to the local militia and took his impressionable boy to military exercises and drills. When America's war with Mexico began in 1846, Armstrong's father could often be heard stating loudly, "My voice is for war!" These words found a place in the young child's mind. Like other boys, Autie probably played with painted toy soldiers. The miniature men with their muskets, swords, horses, and cannons would have sparked his imagination. His stepsister Lydia, who was many years older, sewed him a velvet military uniform. Waving a flag, the

boy marched about for everyone's amusement. He, too, declared loudly, "My voice is for war!" Papa Custer beamed with pride. The smiling onlookers agreed that little George was "a born soldier."

Autie's father said, "I want my boys to be, foremost, soldiers of the Lord." At the Methodist church, Autie learned about the one true God of Christianity; other gods were false gods. Emmanuel "regarded card playing, drinking liquor, dancing, and a host of other pleasures as sinful, did not indulge himself, and was rather successful in keeping his children away from forbidden fruit." As a boy, Autie would have sat in church on Sunday mornings and listened as Bible stories were told about how the first people came into this world. He would have listened with fascination to tales about the creation of night and day and about a great flood that drowned the entire earth. Together with the people of his church he would have sung spiritual songs.

Young Armstrong was athletic—nimble in movement. One of his classmates, R. M. Voorhees, said that Autie did "the hard work of the farm,

A rural one-room school, 1800s. Hand-colored woodcut. Young George Armstrong Custer would have attended school in a classroom much like the one pictured here.

he was a leader in sports, by nature manly, exuberant, enthusiastic." He was quick with a smile and quick to learn. Books stirred his imagination for adventure. He enjoyed reading thrilling stories about heroic soldiers and bold "Indian Fighters." Autie delighted his schoolmates with practical jokes and pranks—flicking paper spit wads across the room or pulling a chair out from under someone. All was done in fun and made him the center of attention. "Custer would always love pranks, a form of humor that combines creativity, energy, and cruelty in nearly equal parts." Armstrong could also awe his fellows with his fearlessness. Once, an older boy sneaked outside the school building. Leering through the window, he made goonish faces at Armstrong, pressing his face against the window in a most irritating manner. Without hesitation,

Autie stepped forward, "smashed his fist through the glass," and delivered a bloody nose. Everyone gasped with astonishment at his sudden impulsive act. With hushed admiration they noted young Custer's demonstration of personal power. Armstrong believed that there was a natural *pecking order*—with dominant individuals at the top and weak ones at the bottom. He decided early on that he would never be at the bottom.

"I am a Lakota of the Oglala band."
—BLACK ELK

The Complete Man

A Lakota boy knew only pure freedom on the open prairies. Schooling did not take place in a square schoolhouse with walls, but beneath a vast blue sky. All boys played games that would someday make them successful buffalo hunters and fierce warriors. "Skinned elbows, knees, and faces . . . were the wounds that turned playful boys into earnest men." A man named Horn Chips remembered, "When we were young, all we thought about was going to war." With bow and arrow, they hunted small birds, gophers, and rabbits. A skilled marksman could shoot a grasshopper! The rabbits were skinned and roasted, making a good meal. Boys developed agility and strength by wrestling, by climbing trees, by chasing each other with saplings for whipping and in games of tag. The boys raced bareback on horses. They tossed mud balls and firebrands at each other, improving their ability to dodge danger. Light Hair was good at all these things. Very good.

Light Hair faced an added challenge—some of the older boys poked fun and called him names for looking different and being small for his age. One of the boys, named Short Bull, would later describe Light Hair's appearance: "His features were not like those of the rest of us. His face was not broad, and he had a sharp, high nose." But Light Hair understood that there existed a pecking order in which the strong boys forced their way to the top and the weaklings were bullied or forced to the bottom. Light Hair had the desire and the athletic ability to stand his ground. He intended to become a true warrior. In a matter of a few years, he was outrunning, outriding, and outshooting the older boys. The teasing and the bullying stopped and were replaced with growing admiration. He "attracted the interest and curiosity" of others.

Another Oglala Lakota, named He Dog, would later say, "We grew up together in the same band, played together, courted the girls together, and fought together."

Late at night, Light Hair would have sat by a campfire with glowing embers and listened as elders told creation stories about how the stars were made and how the first people came into this world. He would have listened with fascination to old stories about how the gift of fire was given to his people, about the Thunder Beings that bring rain, and stories about clever Coyote the Trickster. Together with his people he would have sung ancient songs that celebrated life.

A young man named High Back Bone took notice of the strange boy with quiet determination. He mentored Light Hair, teaching him skills that would build his self-reliance—how to make a sturdy flexible bow and its arrows, a war shield and a stone-headed club. More important, and by his example, he taught Light Hair how to follow the way of the warrior and become a *wica*, a complete man. "The complete man embodied the best qualities of the hunter and the fighting man." He is a man who provides for his family and who as a warrior fights nobly to defend his people in times of danger.

High Back Bone and Light Hair became lifelong friends who joked and laughed. Still, Light Hair preferred being alone. Sometimes he would ride away from the village. He loved looking up at the stars at night. In solitude he could feel the spirit-energy of the earth and sky. Alone, he felt connected to the one Great Spirit in all creation, the one energy that exists within all two-legged beings, or people, and in the four-legged beings (Brothers Coyote, Rabbit, and Deer), in the winged beings of the sky (Brother Hawk, Sisters Raven and Moth), and even in the little creepy-crawlies (Spider and Beetle). The Lakota call this life force the Great Mystery, or Wakan Tanka. Light Hair saw that the world was a place of great

Lakota boys play games to strengthen their skills of riding and shooting.

Black Elk, Oglala Lakota, a medicine man and second cousin of Crazy Horse

beauty with butterfly wings, smiling faces, and deep blue sky above. At the same time, Wakan Tanka—the almighty creator and destroyer—had made this world a place of great danger. In this world there was the hunter and the hunted. Rabbit needed to be wary, for hungry Coyote was ever on the hunt. Deer was always looking over her shoulder, for Mountain Lion needed to eat and feed her growing cubs. Light Hair understood that his Lakota people had to struggle to survive just like the other creatures in this world.

> "The [white man] had found much of the yellow metal
> that they worship and that makes them crazy."
> —BLACK ELK, OGLALA LAKOTA

1848: Gold Is Discovered in California

America was a young and growing nation, expanding its boundaries. Thousands of emigrants, especially young men, flooded westward in the California Gold Rush. Their pursuit of the gleaming yellow treasure took them directly through Indian country, the land the Lakota claimed as their own. In 1849, as this national drama unfolded, ten-year-old Autie moved to Monroe,

Daniel Boone Escorting Settlers Through the Cumberland Gap, *1851–1852 by George Caleb Bingham, captures the essence of the Euro-American's Manifest Destiny to take possession of the continent..*

Michigan, for a brief time to live with Lydia, his married stepsister who had sewn his military uniform years before. Her house would become a second home for Autie. The school he attended continued to shape a growing patriotic view of his country and his place in it. "Autie learned that his country was uniquely blessed, had the finest form of government ever conceived by man, was the freest the world had ever known, and had a Manifest Destiny to overspread the continent." In his mind, the flag of America with its stars and stripes was the most beautiful of flags. Other flags and other groups of people were lesser in importance than his nation.

On summer evenings Autie would have joined the kids in his neighborhood to play tag or hide-and-seek. Their carefree laughter joined with winking fireflies and the stars of night. He took a fancy to girls, and they to him. Autie was still a boy when he met the pretty and intelligent girl who would later become the love of his life. Elizabeth "Libbie" Bacon was about two years younger than Autie, but she caught his eye nonetheless. One day Autie was walking down the street when he ran into Libbie swinging on her front gate. "Hi, you Custer boy!" she called out, grinning, before fleeing into the house. At first the perky girl was not impressed by George Custer. It would take several more years and Armstrong's astonishing heroic deeds in the coming Civil War to change her mind.

The Great Plains—A Land of Brutal Beauty

During the late 1700s, before Light Hair was born, his Lakota people had
been forced from the woodlands of Minnesota by another warring tribe, the
Chippewa/Anishinaabe. But the Lakota were not deterred. Instead, they took
up the gun, learned the art of riding horses, and moved west onto the Great
Plains. The Lakota chief, Red Cloud, would later say, "We moved on our hunting grounds from the Minnesota [River] . . . to the [Rocky Mountains]. No one
put bounds about us."

Before them lay vast grasslands teaming with game—buffalo, antelope, and
deer. In the firmament above, Father Sun burned by day and Sister Moon and
the stars glowed mysteriously by night. The changing seasons tested their will
with winter's blizzards and the searing heat of summer. Dark thunderstorms
could appear suddenly from the west, flaring with lightning and pounding the
earth with hailstones. But the Lakota people adapted. With fierce determination they gained a foothold.

There were seven different bands of Lakota—the Oglala, Hunkpapa, Sicangu,
Mniconju, Oohenunpa, Itazipacola, and Sihasapa. They did not have a single
leader with authority over all, but these nomadic Lakota bands would sometimes come together to celebrate tribal unity. As a sign of their goodwill they
would smoke the sacred pipe, called the chanupa. "As each Indian inhaled the
mixture of Plains tobacco and bearberry kinnikinnick, he offered . . . homage to
the Great Spirit and [attested] that his heart was free from deceit." When necessary, they would unite to fight a common enemy. Light Hair was Oglala Lakota.

The Lakota forced the Crow Indians and other tribes from the Black Hills.

A Shoshonee Indian Smoking, *circa 1858,*
by Alfred Jacob Miller

The Lakota called their new home Paha Sapa. They claimed the surrounding region as their territory. Intertribal battles followed. The Crow, Pawnee, Shoshone, and Rees responded by attacking, stealing horses, and killing Lakota men, women, and children. They had to keep a constant lookout. The vengeful Lakota retaliated by counterattacking and stealing horses from enemy tribes. Boys who had proven themselves to be alert and reliable were given the responsibility of guarding the tribe's horse herd that ranged free outside their village of tipis. They became watchful, cunning, and strong of body. Red Cloud claimed, "When I was young among our nation, I was poor, but from wars with one nation and another I raised myself to be a chief."

There was an ancient Lakota understanding: In order to survive, two-legged beings had to follow the rugged ways of this fierce world. Humans were required to take the life of other creatures in order to eat them and sustain their own life. Hunting and killing were part of that natural order. The Lakota watched how wolf packs hunted the buffalo. They culled out the weak stragglers, the old or the vulnerable young. A lone wolf dared not attack a mighty bull buffalo. But a group of hungry wolves, working together, could take down such a powerful beast. The wolves took turns darting in with slashing fangs. One wolf feigned attack from the front, while another wolf ripped into the prey's blind side. The confused animal would be wounded in the repeated attacks and eventually taken down. The Lakota were like a pack of hungry wolves. Working together empowered them as hunters—and warriors. Black Elk recalled preparing for a buffalo hunt: A man called out, "Your knives shall be sharpened, your arrows

The nomadic Lakota moved their encampments when the natural resources of firewood and game were depleted. They always made camp near water for their horses, dogs, and themselves. Photographer John C. H. Grabill.

shall be sharpened. Make ready, make haste; your horses make ready! We shall go forth with arrows. Plenty of meat we shall make!"

Strangers to the Lakota were potential enemies. They might be viewed with curiosity but were not to be immediately trusted. The Lakota knew to show weakness would surely invite destruction. Aggression needed to be met with aggression, which created ongoing tension and hostility between the Lakota and outsiders. This dynamic is called *tribalism*—a strong loyalty to one's own group: us against them, them against us.

In the years before Light Hair's birth, strange people had started to come up the rivers into Lakota land. They had pale skin. The Lakota called the strangers white men, or *wasichus*. At first, they came with gifts and were looked upon

White Wolves Attacking a Buffalo Bull, *1832–1833, by George Catlin (detail)*

with interest. They came to trade for beaver pelts and buffalo hides. In exchange, they gave the Indians wondrous things—glass beads, metal knives, muskets, sugar, and whiskey. The Lakota joined them in trapping beaver and hunting buffalo.

With the arrival of the wasichus had come an unseen evil force—disease: smallpox, measles, and cholera. The people had no immunity to these foreign diseases that spread with unabated fury. One of the cruelest was smallpox—"a highly contagious disease characterized by chills, pains, and high fever during its initial symptom phase. This phase is followed by the appearance of a skin eruption [blisters] covering the hands and face and, in many cases, the entire body . . . death often occurs suddenly between the fifth and seventh day of illness." Hundreds of thousands died. Entire villages disappeared. Prayers to the sky did not seem to help. Another terrible scourge was brought by the white man—whiskey. Whenever the fur traders started their bartering for buffalo robes, they lubricated the Indians with mind-numbing liquor. The Lakota seemed to have no immunity. Terrible drunkenness and deadly brawls followed. They couldn't get enough and lost all control. Light Hair saw how alcohol took hold of his people. It made them stupid. They traded too many things for more of the liquid poison—buffalo hides, their land, and their spirit. He decided early on not to drink or worship the false god that is found in a bottle.

By the time Light Hair was born, the wasichus had begun coming in greater numbers. Their arrival was stunning. They came up the rivers in steamboats that burned a fire in their belly and belched smoke. The wasichus built roads

Steamboats like the Far West came up the Missouri River with trade items and returned downriver to St. Louis with buffalo robes and animal furs. The animal hides were then transported to cities farther east.

and trading posts; cut down trees, took the land, and pushed the Indians aside. Using muzzle-loading rifles, they slaughtered the buffalo for their hides by the thousands, wiping out entire herds. The Lakota were taken aback and could not allow the slaughter to continue. They depended upon the buffalo for food, clothing, and the lodge coverings for their tipis. The strangers who had come bearing gifts were now seen as an enemy that had come to destroy and conquer. The Hunkpapa warrior Bear's Rib declared, "The whites go wherever they want to . . . Nothing can stop them." If the Lakota were to survive, they would have to fight back. They attacked the wagon trains and settlements of the invaders. The wasichus responded with increased aggression, sending in armed troops, turning their trading posts into forts.

Left: Diseases like measles and cholera spread from village to village by missionaries and traders. Indians who were unknowingly infected transmitted diseases when they visited neighboring villages.

"Progress demanded the conquest of the wilderness . . .
Conquest of the wilderness meant destruction of the Indians."
—ROBERT M. UTLEY

September 1851:
First Fort Laramie Treaty, Wyoming

The U.S. government wanted to end the conflict with the Indians but continue its westward expansion. The government called all the various tribes of Indians on the Northern Great Plains to a meeting at Fort Laramie in order to negotiate a treaty. The Lakota and their allies—the Cheyenne and Arapaho—attended, as well as their enemies—the Crow, Shoshone, Assiniboine, Arikara, Mandan, and Hidatsa. The Pawnee refused to attend out of fear of the Lakota. In the largest assembly of tipis ever witnessed on the Great Plains, nearly ten thousand Indians—men, women, and children—gathered on the prairies surrounding the fort. Their horse herds covered the hills for miles and their campfires lit the night. Drumming and singing reached up to the stars. They had been lured with the promise of gifts—blankets, muskets, coffee, sugar, fabric for clothing, metal utensils, and the like.

The multitude of horses quickly cropped the prairie grass to nubbins. "The entire Indian assembly and the various white commissioners and agents moved about thirty-five miles southeast of the fort to better pasturage near the confluence of the shallow Horse Creek and the North Platte."

The treaty ceremony took place in a great circle. B. G. Brown, a government secretary, described the scene: "Each nation approached with its own peculiar song or demonstration, and such a combination of rude, wild, and fantastic manners and dresses never was witnessed. It is not probable that an opportunity will again be presented of seeing so many tribes . . . exhibiting their wild notions of elegance and propriety."

Historian Stephen Ambrose writes that Light Hair "was about ten years old at the time of the Laramie Council, and one can suppose that he had a marvelous time, riding from camp to camp, getting to know his sworn enemies, meeting Cheyennes, racing on horseback," and competing in other games. "The atmosphere of the council was probably somewhat like that of the county fair eleven-year-old George Custer attended that summer in Ohio, although the Indian council lasted longer."

The government hoped the Indians would sign a peace treaty that would put a stop to intertribal warfare, end the raiding of wagon trains, and permit the safe passage of Americans headed west on the Oregon Trail. The Plains Indians had no centralized Indian "government" like the institutions of the United States. The representatives of the U.S. government were frustrated that they could not negotiate with any designated Indian leaders. They proceeded anyway. They selected chiefs who agreed to put pen to paper. Those who signed the Fort Laramie Treaty promised the peaceful behavior of their people toward the emigrants and all neighboring tribes. In return, the Indians would be given annual presents or supplies worth $50,000 for fifty years. The Senate later reduced the term to fifteen years.

Stu-mick-o-súcks, Buffalo Bull's Back Fat, Head Chief, Blood Tribe, *1832 by George Catlin, shows the magnificent dress and body paint of the typical Plains Indian. Note the scalp lock fringes on his shirt and the large porcupine-quill disk of a thunderbird on his chest.*

Nevertheless, the chiefs chosen by the government could not speak for all the tribes, nor control the behavior of their restless young warriors. Many

Encampment of Piekann Indians, near Fort McKenzie on the Musselshell River, *circa 1840, by Karl Bodmer. The 1851 gathering near Fort Laramie would have looked much like this scene.*

sought personal glory and honor in the traditional aggressive way—the way of the warrior. It was the long-established manner in which young men proved their mettle with daring deeds. They did this by risking their lives, stealing horses from other tribes, and raiding wagon trains and settlements. Young men of any worth aspired to follow this ancient way. One of the most courageous acts that a warrior could perform was called "counting coup." To do this, he had to fearlessly attack an armed enemy, get in close enough to strike the foe with a coup stick or club, then ride his horse away to safety. The warrior did not have to wound the enemy. By simply making contact and dodging away uninjured, he humiliated the opponent and proved himself superior.

"[It is] our manifest destiny to overspread and to possess the whole of the continent which Providence (God) has given us for the development of the great experiment of liberty."
—JOHN L. O'SULLIVAN, American editor
of the *New York Morning News*

August 19, 1854:
The Grattan Fight—Fort Laramie, Wyoming

In the summer of 1854, newspaper articles declared that a deadly fight had taken place on the western frontier between Indians and the U.S. Army. The newspapers called the conflict a *massacre*, or a slaughter of innocent soldiers. Back in Ohio, Autie's father read the news and was outraged. He voiced a need for revenge against the Indians. The teenage Custer heard only his father's version of the story.

At fourteen years of age Light Hair witnessed what happened. His people were camped close to Fort Laramie on the Oregon Trail. They often visited there in order to trade with the wasichus. A lame cow from a passing wagon train strayed near his encampment. A Lakota man shot the animal for food. The wasichu owner of the cow went directly to Fort Laramie and demanded the return of his livestock. Lieutenant John L. Grattan rode out from the fort with an armed force of thirty-one men, pulling two cannons. He demanded that the Lakota chief, Conquering Bear, return the cow and surrender the man who had done the killing. Conquering Bear offered a payment of several healthy horses for the dead cow. Lieutenant Grattan refused the offer. A great crowd of Indians gathered about. The brash officer directed his men to load their cannons and point them at the villagers. Conquering Bear could not bring the cow back to life, he had made a fair offer, and he refused to turn over the man who had killed the animal. Grattan lost all patience with the Lakota people, whom he viewed as

The Grattan Fight

"savages." Someone fired a shot. No one knows which side it came from. The air filled with musket balls and cannon grapeshot. Lakota men, women, and children fell. Conquering Bear lay mortally wounded. The Lakota responded with showers of arrows. Grattan and all his men fell dead. They were scalped and stripped of all their belongings. (It was common practice for the Lakota to mutilate the bodies of their fallen enemies. Doing so left a clear message that they were not to be trifled with. Also, the Lakota believed in life after death. They believed their victims would have to live in the hereafter disfigured for eternity.) There is no account of whether or not Light Hair participated in the fight. But a fourteen-year-old Lakota boy can launch arrows with deadly accuracy.

> "[The boy] dreamed and went into the world
> where there is nothing but the spirits of all things.
> That is the real world that is behind this one."
> —BLACK ELK, OGLALA LAKOTA

1854: The Hanbleceya—Seeking a Vision

Light Hair had grown deeply troubled. The world seemed to be turned on its head. He wanted answers. What was he to do with his life? How was he supposed to serve his people and deal with the looming threat posed by the wasichus? He was no longer a boy, but he was not yet a man.

In Lakota tradition, when a teenage boy is becoming a man he undergoes an ancient ceremony called the Hanbleceya, or Vision Quest. In this rite of passage, the youth goes into the wilderness alone for four days and nights. He fasts—eats no food. He drinks little or no water. He prays to Wakan Tanka for direction in his life. Often the prayers are answered with a profound and holy vision. His father or an elder tells the teenager when it is time to go. In preparation, the boy seeks council from a holy man, a Wichasha Wakan, and is purified in the Inipi, or sweat lodge. Light Hair's father, Tasunke Witco, had taught him about this tradition. But he had not told the boy that his time had come to seek a vision.

Being stubborn and a loner, Light Hair set off on his own. He did not make the traditional preparations. He rode his pinto far from the village. He hobbled his horse near a small lake and climbed the nearby hill. At the summit, Light Hair happened upon a hollow dug in the earth—an eagle-catching pit. Eagle hunters would dig a shallow hole, cover it with branches and dirt, and hide in the pit beneath the covering. For bait, a dead rabbit was laid atop the concealed pit. When an eagle swooped down for a meal of rabbit, the hidden hunter would burst forth with his knife and kill the great bird of prey. The feathers would then be used to create an eagle feather war bonnet.

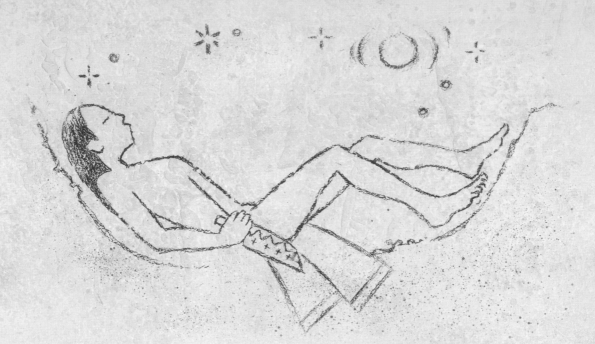

Light Hair crawled into the eagle-catching pit. It seemed like a good place to seek a vision. He lay there all day in the pit, open to the sky. Father Sun passed overhead and darkness fell. Sister Moon rose. The Star People appeared. Light Hair prayed to the one living spirit in all things, Wakan Tanka. The second day came and went, much as the first. The boy felt a gnawing hunger in his stomach and he craved water to moisten his lips. Light Hair felt confused; the stars were overhead again. Was it the second night? Or had he only dreamed of the passing of day? He shifted his body. The boy, not yet a man, sat up. He felt stiffness in his arms and legs. Pebbles had pressed into his back and stuck there. He sat in prayer. Alone with the sun and the moon. He waited. Would a vision ever come? He had hoped a guardian spirit would come to him—maybe a wolf, maybe a spider would speak to him. No spirit came. He grew weary. He knew all too well that he should have asked his father, who was a Wichasha Wakan, for his guidance. He should have purified himself before the glowing firestones in the Inipi. Finally, he stood up. It may have been the third day. He was dizzy; not thinking clearly. Or was it the fourth day? There would be no vision for a strange boy like him.

Light Hair stumbled down the hill toward his hobbled horse near the lake. A dark rain cloud gathered above and seemed to speak with a deep rumbling voice. He had not slept in days and felt disoriented and exhausted. He lost his footing and fell to his knees. As he surrendered, the vision came:

A man on a horse emerged from the waters of the lake, riding toward him. At first, he rode a beautiful bay horse. Then the horse turned into a red sorrel. As the horse with its rider drew near, it changed colors again, becoming a splendid pinto. The powerful animal huffed great drafts of air and its galloping hooves pounded like thunder but did not touch the ground. Lightning flared through pelting rain. The rider wore a single feather and a stone earring. Painted lightning zigzagged down his cheek and chest. His shoulders were colored with hailstones. Bullets cut through the air, but the fearless warrior showed no concern; only determination.

In that moment a red-tailed hawk appeared above the rider. The bird screamed with the power of a thunderbird. The horseman was very close now. He turned his head and spoke without moving his lips. "You have been blessed in the eagle-catching pit. But it is Hawk who will be your spirit brother. Listen to him. He will give you strength. Never wear a war bonnet of Eagle feathers. Never hunt the Eagle, for he is your brother. Wear one Hawk feather and you will be granted the courage of a warrior."* The dream started to fade. The strange rider spoke his parting words. "Live for my people. Keep nothing for yourself." Menacing clouds enveloped the galloping horse and rider. Figures appeared from the shadows, reaching for the rider. They were Lakota people, grabbing the man by his arms, holding him, pulling him from his horse.

*Asterisk denotes not a direct quote.
Following pages: A fierce mounted warrior appeared to Light Hair in a vision.

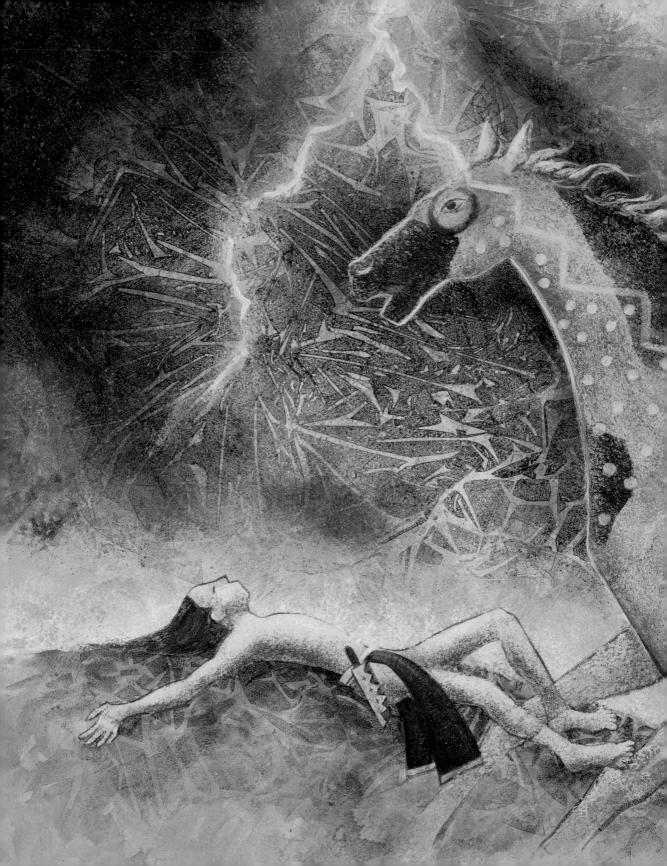

Light Hair lay upon the ground, between dreaming and waking. The passing rain cloud drifted off over the prairie; a flaming rainbow followed close behind. He heard voices calling his name. It was his father, Tasunke Witco, and his friend High Back Bone. His father was angry and scolded, "Where have you been, boy? We've been looking for you for days."* Light Hair raised his head, feeling uncertain and ashamed for venturing out alone. He said nothing. High Back Bone helped him mount his pinto. High above, the red-tailed hawk circled and screamed one last time to acknowledge the great dream. Light Hair did not tell his father or his friend of his vision.

"Stand back, boys; let's have a fair fight."
—GEORGE ARMSTRONG CUSTER

June 1857–June 1861:
West Point, New York

George Custer made friends easily. When he met a girl named Mary Holland they fell headlong, passionately in love. Although the couple was young—Autie was sixteen—they spoke of marriage. The girl's father was not happy about the teenage affair. He looked upon Autie as a youngster without direction or financial standing. Mr. Holland cleverly developed a plan to end the couple's relationship. The man had political connections and helped arrange for Custer to join the military. Armstrong followed through by applying for admittance to the United States Military Academy at West Point. To his astonishment, he was accepted. His boyhood dream of soldiering was coming true. He said goodbye to Mary and traveled east.

As an army cadet, Armstrong often wrote lengthy letters home to Mary, friends, and family. He enjoyed reading, but resisted class work and hated studying for tests. He had no equal when it came to the athleticism needed for horse riding, swordsmanship, and the use of a pistol. All students were trained, in military history, in the tactics of how to command foot soldiers, how to direct cannon fire, how to lead an attack with cavalry and in strategies— how to win a battle. They were schooled in the way of the warrior; very much like their Indian counterparts. For Autie and his friends,

Cadet George Armstrong Custer, age 20, poses with pistol in 1859. Photographer unknown.

however, the tradition harkened back to the days of knighthood and chivalry, to a time when the ideal warrior was revered for his courage, honor, and readiness to defend the weak. The warrior was admired for his willingness to fight and die if necessary. Custer looked admirable in his uniform. But his freewheeling spirit butted against the military discipline that required a proper and structured behavior. Cadets were expected to wake up at a certain time, dress a certain way, eat their meals without talking, go to bed at a certain time, and be absolutely quiet, and on and on . . . These rules rubbed Custer the wrong way. He resisted. When the people in charge weren't looking, he clowned around. And his classmates genuinely liked him for his rascal behavior.

Cadets at West Point Military Academy, New York, circa 1860s. Photographer unknown.

His roommate Tully McCrea said, "He is always connected with all the mischief that is going on and never studies any more than he can possibly help. He has narrowly escaped several times." McCrea went on to say, "He is a handsome fellow, and a very successful ladies' man." One night, Armstrong and a few other cadets sneaked from their barracks after "lights out." They slipped past the sentries to attend a Thanksgiving party in town where they danced and mingled with young ladies late into the night. In a letter to his cousin, Augusta Ward, Custer described the regrettable effects of going the night without sleep. "[We] reached home a few minutes before reveille [at 5:00 a.m.], changed our citizen's dress for our uniforms, and were then safe. I was in poor humor for hard study during the next day . . . and under the circumstances I was almost (*but not quite*) sorry I had gone to the ball."

Custer regularly received demerits for "boyish conduct" during class or military drills, for wearing an untidy uniform or for prankish misconduct toward fellow cadets. Armstrong racked up more demerits than any other cadet. His punishment usually resulted in endless hours of marching alone in uniform, in silence. Still, his infectious laughter and adventurous spirit made him a popular fellow among his peers. His classmate Peter Michie recalled, "Custer . . . was always in trouble with the authorities . . . He had more fun, gave his friends more anxiety, walked more tours of extra guard, and came nearer to being dismissed more often than any other cadet I have ever known."

Because he was self-assured and comfortable with himself, others looked up to him as a natural leader. Contradictions in Armstrong's character became apparent while he was at the military academy. To a certain degree he liked the structure of the military, but he did not necessarily like obeying the rules himself. During his senior year he was called to trial by his commanders. He was court-martialed for not breaking up a fistfight between two younger cadets. It had been his duty to keep order. Instead he egged on the fighters, much to his classmates' entertainment. Autie needed to accept the

strange paradox: The war college was training the cadets to be fighters and yet it forbade fighting.

The military court found him guilty of "Neglect of Duty" and "Conduct to the prejudice of good order and Military discipline." Custer was lucky he was not kicked out of the academy. He was like a spirited young horse that did not like the steel bit in his mouth or the saddle on his back. Nonetheless, his experiences at the military academy at West Point gave shape to the boy who was becoming a man.

When Custer misbehaved, he often did so at great risk to himself. But his fellow cadets were captivated by his devil-may-care attitude and defiance of the rules. Armstrong enjoyed, actually reveled in, being the center of attention. When he misbehaved, he demonstrated a willingness to take risks that none of his classmates dared consider. Soon he would be taking death-defying risks that would catapult him to glorious national fame.

"They would ride right up to a bison and shoot him behind the left shoulder. Some of the arrows would go in up to the feathers and sometimes those that struck no bones went right straight through."
—BLACK ELK, OGLALA LAKOTA

Hunting Buffalo and Telling the Truth

Light Hair and a friend named Lone Bear joined with the men of their tribe in hunting the buffalo. At first, they did not actually hunt. They helped drive the moving herds of buffalo—they rode their horses along the edge of stampeding herds, waving a blanket overhead. In this way they kept hundreds of panicked buffalo together, making them an easier target for the hunters carrying spears and bows and arrows. In time they were asked to join in the actual hunt—a dangerous undertaking. But Light Hair and Lone Bear were up to the task. Their

Buffalo Hunt, Chase, *by George Catlin, 1844*

Water is poured upon the sacred heated stones during the Inipi ceremony.

horsemanship was exceptional. They could maneuver their horses next to one of the massive lunging beasts, loosing arrows as they went, then gallop away to safety as the buffalo fell.

More than a year had passed since Light Hair's extraordinary vision. He had told no one. He thought about it often, but he felt ashamed that he had gone alone without permission or the traditional preparation. Tasunke Witco could see that Light Hair was becoming a successful hunter and growing into a man. He told Light Hair that it was time to prepare for his Hanbleceya. Light Hair could no longer keep his secret. He admitted that he had broken tradition and sought a vision without permission and the proper blessing. His father could have reacted with anger. Instead, Tasunke Witco responded with understanding. He made arrangements for an Inipi ceremony.

Inside the circle of the lodge, Light Hair sat with the men of his tribe. His friend High Back Bone was there, too. Large stones that had been heated in a fire outside were brought in and stacked in a central pit. The door flap was closed, shutting out all daylight. In the pitch darkness the "Stone People" glowed fiery red and radiated intense heat. Light Hair could just make out the facial features and forms of those who sat across from him. Tasunke Witco sprinkled sage leaves on the Stone People and a sweet-smelling smoke rose, filling the lodge with purifying incense. The holy man poured water that struck the fiery stones and erupted with an explosive clap. Searing steam filled the lodge. Someone began pounding a rawhide drum; a gourd rattle joined in rhythm and ancient songs were sung. Condensing water flowed over Light Hair's body—cleansing and purifying. His father asked for a blessing from Wakan Tanka and then called upon his son to speak.

Light Hair shared the story of his time in the eagle-catching pit. He spoke of the strange rider on the horse of many colors and the red-tailed hawk. The holy man sat thoughtfully for a long time, then interpreted and explained the vision. He told Light Hair that Wakan Tanka had called him for a holy vision; that it was right for him to go alone to that high place with the eagle-catching pit. Sometimes, traditions needed to be set aside and a person needed to follow their heart. A great gift had been given to him. Tasunke Witco told Light Hair that the rider in the vision was actually him. He said that Light Hair was to serve his people as a warrior and that he would be guided in life by the spirit of Brother Hawk. Tasunke Witco said that his rite of passage from boyhood to manhood was nearing completion. It would be tested and made final in battle with the enemy.

> "Crazy Horse charged . . . right into the Crows and
> fought them back with only a bow and arrows."
> —BLACK ELK, OGLALA LAKOTA

1858: Wind River, Wyoming

The Lakota continued to raid wagon trains and white settlements and to steal horses and fight with other tribes on the high plains. Light Hair regularly fought in these encounters and honed his skills as a warrior. One of his companions, Eagle Elk, told of the time during a raid against the Pawnee when Light Hair "was just a very young boy." He was shot through the arm while attacking the enemy. "From that time," Eagle Elk said, "he was talked about" with admiration. According to author Joseph M. Marshall, when Light Hair rode into battle, he "stripped to his breechclout and moccasins, his hair loose in the manner of his dream and the lightning mark and hailstones painted on his chest. At the back of his head he wore the tail [feather] from a red-tailed hawk . . . In his right hand he held the bow, two arrows against his palm and a third clamped in his teeth." In another fight, with the Arapaho, he put an arrow into an enemy's ribs and took his scalp. He put another arrow in a second foe. But after he dismounted and scalped the man, everything went wrong. At that moment his horse bolted away and he was struck in the leg with an Arapaho arrow. His friend High Back Bone rode to the rescue, pulling him to safety on the back of his horse. High Back Bone pulled out the arrow and helped bandage Light Hair's wound.

After such skirmishes the Lakota would return to their village and celebrate a victory. All the women and girls made the high-pitched trilling sound, which is made by singing out while vibrating the tongue. Fellow warriors cheered Light Hair's fearlessness. His father came to recognize the maturity and courageous heart of his son. To honor him, Tasunke Witco gave the teenager his own name. It was common practice among the Lakota for a father to pass along his own name to a respected son. The man declared for all to hear, "I give my first son a new name this day . . . I give him the name of his father and of his fathers before him. From this day forward I call him Crazy Horse!" The holy man would also take a new name—Waglula, which means Worm. Loosely translated, Tasunke Witco means a spirited horse that stomps its hooves, rears up, and can never be tamed. Ever after, Light Hair would be known as Tasunke Witco—Crazy Horse.

Light Hair is given the name Tasunke Witco, "Crazy Horse."

"We hold these truths to be self-evident, that all men are created equal, that they are endowed by their Creator with certain unalienable Rights, that among these are Life, Liberty and the pursuit of Happiness."
—United States Declaration of Independence,
July 4, 1776

1861: War and Manhood

Far away in the East, American society was being torn apart by a political disagreement over the question of slavery. In the northern states, workers were paid wages for their labor in an economy driven by manufacturing and industrialization. In the southern states, with its agricultural economy, white people owned black people as property and forced them to work and paid them no wages. Millions of human beings suffered under the grinding boot of slavery. Abraham Lincoln, the presidential candidate from the northern states, was an abolitionist. Along with others, he wanted to abolish slavery. He stood by the words of the Declaration of Independence, which clearly states, "*All men are created equal.*"

President Abraham Lincoln, 1869, engraving based on a photograph by Matthew Brady

Supporters of slavery hated Lincoln's interpretation of the words. They believed people of color were not really "men," and they certainly weren't "equal." This included the Indians, too. After Lincoln's election in 1860, eleven southern states revolted and seceded from the United States of America. They formed a new country under a new flag—the Confederate States of America. In April 1861, they declared war against the United States!

Cadet Custer had become good friends with many of his classmates. Several had grown up in the southern states and supported the cruel idea of slavery. They dropped out of the academy before graduation and joined the Confederate Army to fight against the United States. In a letter to his sister, Custer wrote, "You cannot imagine how sorry I will be to see this happen, as the majority of my best friends and all my room mates except one have been from the South." Although Custer supported the idea of slavery and of white supremacy, he remained loyal to the Union. He believed the secessionists from the southern states were traitors. The Confederacy immediately began to amass a great

An African American brother and sister, formerly enslaved, hold hands, 1864, photograph by P.F. Cooper.

army in the South. The regular army in the North did not have enough soldiers needed to defeat the Rebels. "Lincoln asked for 75,000 militiamen to put down the South's rebellion. The North responded with mobs of [eager] volunteers . . . from Iowa to Maine." It was up to individual states to organize these groups of militiamen.

"Such state-organized units, known as the U.S. Volunteers, formed the vast bulk of the forces that would prosecute the war, yet they remained organizationally separate from the standing Regular Army." Volunteers did not have the same training and combat readiness of the Regulars. Custer knew that he might receive a higher rank more quickly in the Michigan Volunteers. He stated, "I would prefer serving with the troops of my native state. Besides . . . I could be certain of being at least a Captain and probably higher."

Custer could not wait to join in the fight. "It is my great expectation to fight for my country," he wrote his sister, "and to die for it if need be. The thought has often occurred to me that I might be killed in this war; and if so, so be it." In June 1861, a new class of smartly dressed cadets graduated from West Point. Young Custer's grades were far from the best: "He ranked thirty-fourth in a class of thirty-four." He was commissioned as a second lieutenant in the Union Army. In his mind, the rank affirmed his passage into manhood. The twenty-one-year-old was eager and ready for war!

> "Crazy Horse always led his men himself
> when they went into battle, and he kept well in front of them."
> —HE DOG, OGLALA LAKOTA

Meeting Aggression with Aggression

Meanwhile, the aggressive invasion of emigrants into Lakota lands continued. Black Elk remembered, "The Wasichus had found much of the yellow metal that they worship and that makes them crazy, and they wanted to have a road up through our country to the place where the yellow metal was." The U.S. government and the newspapers declared there was gold and land free for the taking. The Lakota held their ground. They met aggression with aggression. It was either *us or them—them or us*. Across the Great Plains, Indian raids increased. Crazy Horse joined other warriors who attacked the white intruders. His fellow warrior He Dog said, "He was a very quiet man except when there was fighting." Facing off against an enemy gave him a thrill and exhilaration like no other. Crazy Horse always rode to the front of the fight. Like the rider in his vision, he fought with no fear of being struck by the bullets that cut through the air. Under heavy rifle fire, Crazy Horse would dismount to steady his shooting (a courageous act for any horseman). With feet planted firmly on the ground he took careful aim,

Pawnee Indians Watching the Caravan, *circa 1837, by Alfred Jacob Miller*

Crazy Horse charges ahead and men follow him.

killing many. Crazy Horse's reputation as an enemy-killer grew. He had a force protecting him—the divine power of Wakan Tanka! He gathered a following. Crazy Horse's men believed he possessed a power over death, a kind of immortality. He led by individual example. He did not give orders. Crazy Horse simply charged ahead and men followed him. Together they raided the vulnerable wagon trains to steal horses, rifles, ammunition, blankets, and any of the treasures brought by the wasichus. The public became enraged and demanded military protection from the Indians.

> "Oh, could you but have seen some of the charges that were made!
> While thinking of them I cannot but exclaim 'Glorious War!'"
> —GEORGE ARMSTRONG CUSTER, 1863

1861–1865: The American Civil War

Custer received orders to report to army headquarters in Washington, D.C. There he was given urgent dispatches to be delivered to the commander on the front lines near Manassas, Virginia. Thousands of Northern soldiers faced off against thousands of Southern rebel soldiers on the banks of Bull Run Creek. Muskets blasted, cannons roared, men and their horses fell. The devastating fire of musket balls from the Confederate Army forced the Union men to fall back in retreat. A stunned Armstrong was left with no reasonable choice but to join the beaten Union soldiers as they withdrew from the field of battle. He

This preliminary drawing for the painting Skirmish Line, *circa 1880s, by Gilbert Gaul, depicts a frontline of Union riflemen in battle.*

felt humiliated by the gray-uniformed enemy and would do all in his power to prevent such a defeat from happening again.

In another conflict, the Union Army came upon the Chickahominy River. The enemy held ground on the other side. This time Custer led "thirty men from the 4th Michigan" downriver and crossed in a flanking maneuver. Custer's infantrymen advanced on foot and came in behind the rebels. Through the trees he could see their battle flags, gray jackets, and faces. His blood was up. "Custer fired first, igniting a volley from his men. The enemy scrambled about in confusion" and fell back. They were either shot dead, wounded, or fled in disarray. His superior reported, "Lieutenant Custer was the first to cross the stream, the first to open fire upon the enemy, and one of the last to leave the field." Many battles followed. Armstrong slashed men with his sword and shot them with his pistol. With a fearless heart he always led the charge. For him battle played out like a game, a *very* intense game in which men on the losing team died. According to historian Paul Hutton, "George Armstrong Custer loved war. It was as a tonic to him. Whereas others shrank from its ghastly carnage, he reveled in it."

> "My dear 'Beloved Star'—You could not have given me anything
> on earth that so delighted me—except yourself."
> —Letter from ELIZABETH "LIBBIE" BACON to
> GEORGE "AUTIE" CUSTER, December 23, 1863,
> from Monroe, Michigan

November 1862: Love and War

For his bravery, Armstrong was promoted to the brevet rank of captain (brevet ranks were temporary wartime positions awarded to U.S. Volunteers). He was given leave from battle on the front lines. Custer returned to his second home in Monroe, Michigan, to be with his stepsister Lydia and her family. He received a warm welcome. The handsome cavalryman presented a striking image in his officer's uniform. The young bachelor attended parties and other social gatherings. Armstrong became socially reacquainted with Libbie Bacon, whom he had known as a boy. Libbie was intelligent and beautiful—the most sought-after and eligible young woman in town. Evenings included dancing, singing around a piano, gossiping, drinking, and laughing. Sometimes, Custer's drinking got out of control. In one incident, Custer's rowdy cavorting created a public scene witnessed by Libbie and her disapproving father. About town, people gossiped openly about his wild behavior. Armstrong realized that the intoxicating effect of liquor damaged his reputation. Drunkenness would destroy his standing in the military and wreck any chance of courtship with the

George Armstrong Custer. The one star on
his collar and epaulet represents the rank
of brevet brigadier general.

Elizabeth "Libbie" Bacon

charming Libbie Bacon. He decided he would never drink again. He never did.

When Armstrong returned to the battlefront he and Libbie wrote lengthy letters to each other. But he kept his focus on being a commander. Captain Custer participated in many battles—the Maryland Campaign, the Battle of South Mountain, and the Battle of Antietam, to name a few. On June 17, 1863, near the village of Aldie, Virginia, Custer led the 1st Maine Cavalry in a charge. Mounted on his black horse, he "plunged into the onrushing mass of enemy cavalry. One Confederate swiveled and fired his revolver; Custer swung his sword and cut almost all the way through the man's arm. Another rebel, saber in hand, galloped after Custer from behind . . . Custer beat down the rebel's sword and finally cut into his skull and brain."

The saber was the weapon of choice for cavalrymen. Muzzle-loading muskets were too cumbersome for a man in the saddle, and pistols could be held in one hand but at some point, they needed reloading. Sabers on the other hand were always at the ready. The typical army issue saber had a thirty-three-inch-long blade—excellent for slashing and stabbing. In close quarters the long reach of Armstrong's blade was absolutely murderous.

Time and again Custer demonstrated to those around him and in particular to his superior officer, Major General Alfred Pleasonton, that he was a leader of men. When he led a company of cavalry toward the Confederates, with their sabers drawn, it got the enemy's attention. Armstrong had a genuine affection for all of the men in the Cavalry Corps. As an officer on Pleasonton's staff, he helped ensure that they were well fed, that they had the best equipment and healthy horses. In turn, his men came to admire their long-haired captain for his gallantry and death-defying courage. Major James Harvey Kidd of the

6th Michigan Cavalry would later declare, "We swear by him. His name is our battle cry. He Can get twice the fight out of this brigade that any other man Can possibly do." And, "Under him a man is ashamed to be Cowardly. Under him our men can achieve wonders."

George Armstrong Custer presents a strikingly handsome figure.

His many victories earned him national attention. Newspaper reporters wrote articles that praised his success on the battlefield. The American public relished the detailed stories about the young bold warrior-hero with long golden hair. The army desperately needed officers who could win fights against the rebels. For his feats of extraordinary courage, Custer was promoted to the brevet rank of a one-star brigadier general in the U.S. Volunteers. At twenty-three years of age he became the youngest general in the Union forces. Autie relished the adulation and status of being a national celebrity. With chin up and shoulders back, he dressed for the part—a broad-brimmed hat, a black velvet jacket with brass buttons, and a long red scarf. The public wanted a performance and he gave them one.

Major General Pleasonton reorganized the Cavalry Corps and named it the 3rd Cavalry Division. He gave Custer command of the Michigan Brigade, which included the 1st, 5th, 6th, and 7th Michigan Cavalry, approximately 1,700 men. They called themselves the Wolverines.

Following pages: Captain Custer's charges inspired his men.

> "I hope and trust that strength will be given to me to stand and do my duty."
> —PRIVATE EDWARD EDES, in a letter to his father, April 1863

July 1–3, 1863—
The Battle of Gettysburg, Pennsylvania

The opposing armies met beneath a hot July sun at the crossroads of a small Pennsylvania farm town—Gettysburg. More than 90,000 Union soldiers massed against approximately 70,000 Confederates. The immense assembly of men in blue and gray uniforms moved in formations with horse-drawn cannons. Each regiment displayed their colorful battle flags, while marching bands played rousing tunes, lending an air of pageantry to the scene. The battle would rage for three days, and thousands would give their lives in a terrible glory. Cannons boomed from a mile away, hurling long-range twelve-pound iron balls and exploding projectiles that ripped and shredded. As the opposing armies drew closer, the big field guns launched short-range canisters of grape-shot that pummeled rows of men with more than twenty balls of lead at one time, maiming and killing with horrific effect. Drums beat and bugles called above the gunsmoke-filled turmoil. Advancing shoulder to shoulder, rows of marching men crumpled beneath a hailstorm of lead musket balls and shrapnel. There were desertions in the face of the unfolding horror. Some threw down their weapons; their trembling legs would no longer carry them forward. They turned and ran. Still the armies advanced. Both sides planned to defeat the enemy or go down fighting. Onward into the slaughter yard they pressed their attack, tramping over the dead and dismembered. There were battles within battles—mad confusion, where men driven by primal instinct fought hand to hand. The soldiers on both sides no longer gave thought to the rightness or wrongness of slavery. Instead, they fought because it was their duty to their country. Others fought because they hated the enemy. The righteous fought for their god. Others fought for their brothers in arms. To turn and run would bring dishonor and shame. Those who fell gave their lives for a higher good—for their tribe. Their sacrifice would be remembered as a holy act of martyrdom.

In midafternoon on the third day of the battle an overwhelming force of Confederates tried to outflank the Union cavalry. "A grander spectacle than their advance has rarely been beheld," one Union cavalryman wrote. "They marched with well-aligned fronts and steady reins. Their polished saber-blades dazzled in the sun. All eyes turned upon them." The order was given to "charge" and "on came the rebel cavalry, yelling like demons." But General Custer knew how to stop the attack. He rode to the front of the 1st Michigan Cavalry regiment and redirected them in a counterattack. With his sword flashing, he commanded, "Come on, you Wolverines!" The Union cavalry plowed into the enemy head on, "sabering all who came within reach," Custer recalled. "So sudden and violent was the collision," another witness stated, "that many of the horses were turned end over end and crushed the riders beneath them." The horrible roar of yelling human beings, screaming horses, and hammering musket-fire inspired Custer with a heart-pounding rush.

The young general's horse "took a bullet to the foreleg, and staggered and fell. Custer got clear, pulled himself onto a riderless horse, and rejoined the fight." Armstrong later reported, "For a moment, but only a moment, that long, heavy column stood its ground; then, unable to withstand the impetuosity of our attack, it gave way into a disorderly rout." Together, Custer and his men outmaneuvered and pushed back the enemy. His fearless leadership helped to change the outcome of the battle into a victory.

Following pages: The Battle of Gettysburg: Repulse of Longstreet's Assault, July 3, 1863, 1870 by James Walker

Teams of horses and mules pulled wagons called caissons loaded with cannonballs and gunpowder. Thousands were killed on the battlefield.

The aftermath was a hellish scene of carnage—thousands of dead men, some with dull open eyes that stared into the nothingness that is death. Scattered among them lay ruined wagons, muskets, swords, broken flags, and countless dead horses. The putrid smell turned stomachs. So many gave their blood and lives upon the battlefield that to this day Gettysburg is honored as holy ground, a sacred place. The battle was the turning point of the war and portended the defeat of the Confederacy. Many more battles followed.

Right: More than seven thousand men died and more than thirty thousand were wounded at the battle of Gettysburg. By war's end 620,000 would give their lives.

"When I think how successful I have been of late and
how much has been said of my conduct and gallantry I think,
'She will hear of it and will be proud of her Boy!'
That is all the reward I ask."
—GEORGE CUSTER, in a letter to
ELIZABETH BACON, May 1864, from Virginia

Hail the Hero

Custer's bravery and good luck became legendary. He would ride headlong into battle while men and horses fell in death on his right and left. In fact, he had more horses shot out from under him than seems possible—by war's end, eleven. In the turmoil of battle, he would find a riderless horse, mount up, and fight on. He "received bullet holes in his hat, had a lock of his hair cut off by a passing shot [and] was wounded in the thigh by a spent ball." Facing death and cheating death thrilled him with an exhilarating joy! The Northern newspapers hailed him as the "Boy General of the Golden Locks."

Back in Monroe, Michigan, Libbie Bacon read all the newspaper accounts of Armstrong's exploits. She also read the many letters he sent her. Autie took another leave from battle and returned home. On February 9, 1864, the two were married. By the war's end, the heroic young general had been promoted to the brevet rank of a two-star major general. "Custer" had become a household name, known to everyone. Armstrong understood that his celebrity status gave him fame that could lead to riches and more power, even to the office of presidency of the United States. He reinforced his notoriety with newspaper articles, stories that were embellished with the new technological development—photography. More photographs were taken of him than of President Lincoln.

General George Armstrong Custer and his wife,
Elizabeth "Libbie" Bacon Custer

A shirt like the one awarded to Crazy Horse, honoring him as a "Shirt Wearer"—a chief among the Lakota ca. 1870s

> "When we were made chiefs,
> we were bound by very strict rules ...
> I have always kept the oaths I made then,
> but Crazy Horse did not."
> —HE DOG, OGLALA LAKOTA

1865: Crazy Horse Is Made a Shirt Wearer

The bourgeoning age of photography enveloped the Native population as well. Many people sat for photographers. Crazy Horse, on the other hand, was never photographed. He refused to let a photographer lure him into his studio and capture his *medicine spirit* with a black-and-white image on paper. He reportedly said, "Why would you want to take from me my shadow?" His appearance remains a mystery. Still, Black Elk knew him well and left this description: "He was a small man among the Lakotas and he was slender and had a thin face and his eyes looked through things and he always seemed to be thinking hard about something." Also, unlike other chiefs such as Red Cloud and Sitting Bull, Crazy Horse left no signature. He never put pen to paper and he never signed a treaty with the white man.

As the years passed, the chiefs among the Oglala grew to admire Crazy Horse's good judgment and fearless leadership. When he was about twenty-five, they honored the young warrior by proclaiming him to be "Shirt Wearer"—a respected position of authority, a chief. The young Tasunke Witco was given a handsome shirt made from bighorn sheep skins, decorated with dyed porcupine quills and fringed with human scalp locks. The entire village gathered for the celebration. All the women and girls made the trilling sound.

Crazy Horse took notice of young women in his village. There was one in particular whom he fancied—Black Buffalo Woman. But her family married her to a man named No Water. He was a successful hunter who had his own lodge and could provide for her. Sometimes No Water would be gone from the village, either buffalo hunting or warring against an enemy. During such absences, Crazy Horse would meet secretly with Black Buffalo Woman. Upon returning from a horse-stealing raid, No Water barged in on them and shot Crazy Horse in the face with a pistol. Amazingly, the bullet entered his cheek and glanced out his upper jaw by the ear. It took months for the wound to heal. His face would bear the scar of his misdeed. The elders of the tribe agreed that Tasunke Witco should be disciplined for his affair with Black Buffalo Woman. Crazy Horse had shown poor judgment and acted selfishly. They removed his status as a Shirt Wearer and chief. His humiliation was great, for he had placed his personal desires before the needs of his people.

Crazy Horse was not one to surrender to his enemies or to the shame of his own mistakes. Seasons passed. He fell in love again and married, this time with a young woman named Black Shawl. Together they had a child, a girl they named They Are Afraid of Her. It was an unusual name for a baby girl. Crazy Horse hoped the name would help ward off the dangers surrounding her in this world. Most fathers preferred having a boy child, one who would become a warrior. But the bond of love grew between Crazy Horse and his daughter. The girl's innocent smile and the way she toddled about charmed the heart of the fierce Lakota warrior.

> "This is a country for white men, and, by God,
> as long as I am President, it shall be a government for white men."
> —PRESIDENT ANDREW JOHNSON

Reconstruction in the South:
White Against Black

After four years of fighting and with the staggering loss of 620,000 lives, the brutal Civil War came to an end. The United States of America defeated the Confederate States of America and preserved the Union. The commander of their army, General Robert E. Lee, surrendered to the commander of the Union Army, General Ulysses S. Grant, on April 9, 1865, in a farmhouse in Appomattox, Virginia. Major General G. A. Custer, along with other officers, was in attendance outside. Slavery was outlawed on paper. Nevertheless, racial hatred and the terrible mistreatment of blacks continued.

John Wilkes Booth assassinates President Lincoln.

John Wilkes Booth, a Confederate sympathizer, refused to accept defeat. On the night of April 14, five days after the official surrender, President Abraham Lincoln attended a performance at Ford's Theatre with his wife, Mary. In the dark, Booth sneaked in behind the unsuspecting couple and shot Lincoln in the back of the head. He died the next day. Vice President Andrew Johnson became the next president. Unlike Lincoln, he believed blacks were inferior to white people. He said, "White men alone must manage the South." He issued a series of proclamations that supported a set of "black codes" that "largely restricted African Americans to working for their old masters."

The war was supposed to be over, but fighting continued in Southern states and the Confederate State of Texas refused to surrender. Texas was committed to enslaving black people. "In 1860, there had been 275,000 slaves in Texas, about a third of the state population; by 1865 the number had risen to 400,000." Custer was given command of five cavalry regiments and was sent to Texas to establish order. The rebel army of Texas gave up and disbanded before his arrival. Custer would spend the better part of the next year as a commander of Federal troops assigned to the task of Reconstruction in the South. His wife, Libbie, accompanied him. While in the South, they attended many social gatherings and befriended the wealthy white plantation owners and other people of high society. Custer opposed slavery, but at the same time he agreed with the view that whites were superior. He made this clear when he wrote, "I am in favor of elevating the negro to the extent of his capability and intelligence . . . but in making this advancement I am opposed to doing it by correspondingly reducing or debasing any portion of the white race." As commander of the Federal troops after the war he did little to ensure the fair and safe treatment of African Americans. Still, he witnessed racist behavior and reported in writing that black people were still being bought and sold and that many of those who resisted were murdered. Custer stated, "A system of oppression is being inaugurated throughout this state upon the part of the former owners against the Freedman [former enslaved people]."

Custer chose to side with the privileged white class and to discount people of color. He struggled with his personal "contradictory impulses and convictions." Other citizens saw the situation with greater clarity and were outraged by the repulsive and murderous treatment of blacks. Benjamin Brisbane, chaplain of the 2nd Wisconsin, wrote from Texas, "The freedmen in this section are in a very unsatisfactory condition, and the military authorities instead of aiding them are allowing the old masters to impose upon them . . . Many have been shot because they would not sign an agreement to work for little or nothing." The provisional governor of Texas, Andrew J. Hamilton, stated, "There is scarcely a day that I am not informed of a homicide committed upon a Freedman." Racism, with its hostility toward blacks and tribal resentment of Northerners continued. Many in the South persisted in defiantly flying the flag of the Confederate States of America. Tyrannical "black codes" became the norm—blacks would be segregated from whites.

"I am convinced that somehow we must whip these Indians terribly to make them fear & respect us."
—GENERAL WILLIAM TECUMSEH SHERMAN

The U.S. Army vs. the American Indians for Control of the Great Plains

Racial hatred and its version of tribalism was not limited to freed blacks but also included Indians and other groups. At war's end, the military reduced its numbers. Most soldiers were happy to go home to civilian life, but Custer intended to make soldiering his life's career. His brevet rank as a two-star general was a wartime position. On July 28, 1866, Custer was appointed lieutenant colonel of the newly created 7th Cavalry Regiment. The nation turned its attention to the Far West.

During the war Congress had passed the Homestead Act of 1862. According to its terms "any U.S. citizen or alien immigrant could claim 160 acres" of western land referred to as public domain. All they had to do was pay a $10 filing fee and "live on the land and farm it for five years." The word that 160 acres of land was basically free and up for grabs spread like wildfire. Newspapers gave voice to the belief in Manifest Destiny and the right to disregard the Indians, cut the timber, mine for minerals, and farm the land. Wagon trains had already been headed for California and Montana, where gold had been discovered. Now there was a land rush. More settlers, miners, buffalo robe hunters, merchants, and missionaries traveled the Oregon and Bozeman Trails, which crossed the country. The Euro-Americans thought the great expanse of land was theirs for the taking, and they had the power to take it.

Every year thousands of Euro-Americans traveled through Indian country along the Oregon Trail, which went from the Missouri River to what is now the state of Oregon. The migrants included settlers, farmers, miners, ranchers, and business owners and their families. Pictorial Press Ltd/Alamy.

> "I want to know what you are doing traveling on this road.
> You scare all the buffalo away. I want to hunt on the place.
> I want you to turn back from here.
> If you don't, I will fight you again."
> —SITTING BULL, HUNKPAPA LAKOTA

A Change of Tactics

The Indians who had lived freely on the land for generations retaliated against the intruders by continuing to raid wagon trains, settlements, and trading posts, killing and burning as they went.

The U.S. Army responded by building three new forts along the Bozeman Trail—Fort Reno, Fort Phil Kearny, and Fort C. F. Smith. Soldiers patrolled the surrounding areas and protected the white newcomers. The Lakota were

Chief Red Cloud, Makhpiya-luta, Oglala Lakota

infuriated by the forts on their land. The Crow Indians were happy to have the forts; they had been forced from the Black Hills and surrounding area by the Lakota. The Crow joined forces with the army, hoping to regain their buffalo hunting grounds. Their warriors acted as scouts for the bluecoats— the name given to the soldiers because of their blue uniforms.

Lakota chief Red Cloud, along with warriors like Crazy Horse, were fighting for their people and the territory they claimed as theirs. Red Cloud devised a strategy to stop the wasichus. The plan required a new approach to fighting. Red Cloud organized the nomadic Lakota bands into a united force that would follow his orders. Cheyenne allies joined the Lakota in the effort. Even the Arapaho, now friends, joined the Lakota. Together they killed scores of bluecoats and emigrants, stole horses and cattle, and put a complete stop to travel on the Bozeman Trail.

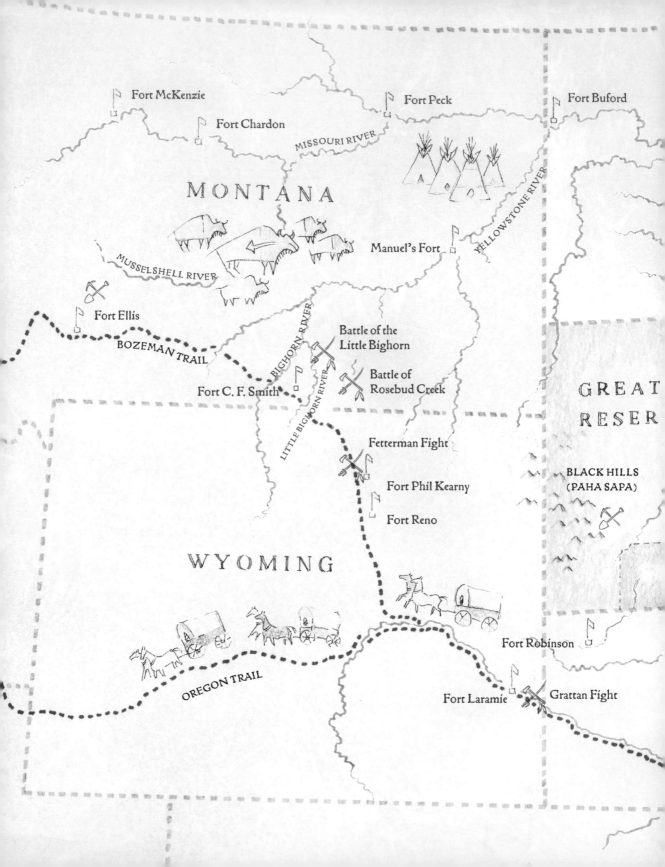

Fort McKenzie

Fort Chardon

Fort Peck

Fort Buford

MISSOURI RIVER

MONTANA

YELLOWSTONE RIVER

Manuel's Fort

MUSSELSHELL RIVER

Fort Ellis

BIGHORN RIVER

BOZEMAN TRAIL

Battle of the
Little Bighorn

Fort C. F. Smith

LITTLE BIGHORN RIVER

Battle of
Rosebud Creek

GREAT

RESER

Fetterman Fight

BLACK HILLS
(PAHA SAPA)

Fort Phil Kearny

Fort Reno

WYOMING

Fort Robinson

OREGON TRAIL

Fort Laramie

Grattan Fight

GREAT PLAINS

NORTH DAKOTA

KNIFE RIVER

Fort Lincoln

HEART RIVER

Fort Rice

CANNONBALL RIVER

Fort Yates

STANDING ROCK INDIAN RESERVATION

GRAND RIVER

SIOUX VATION

SOUTH DAKOTA

CHEYENNE RIVER

Fort Pierre

MISSOURI RIVER

WHITE RIVER

PINE RIDGE INDIAN RESERVATION

Fort Randall

RED RIVER OF THE NORTH

MINNESOTA

IOWA

N
W — E
S

Battlefields

Forts

Goldfields

*State borders reflect today's boundaries.

NIOBRARA RIVER

NEBRASKA

GREAT PLAINS

NORTH PLATTE RIVER

> "Give me eighty men and I would ride through
> the whole Sioux nation."
> —CAPTAIN WILLIAM J. FETTERMAN

December 21, 1866: The Battle of the Hundred-in-the-Hand or The Fetterman Fight— Fort Phil Kearny, Wyoming

The winter sun made its passage low in the sky. Snow melted on the ridges, but lay frozen in shadowed ravines. Woodcutters ventured out from Fort Phil Kearny with wagons to gather firewood and timber for fort construction. They were only a few miles from the fort when Crazy Horse led a small band of Lakota against them, not an uncommon event.

A force of eighty cavalry and infantry headed out from the fort, under the command of Captain William J. Fetterman, to rescue the woodcutters. He was

The Fetterman Massacre or the Battle of the Hundred-in-the-Hand. Lakota and Cheyenne warriors battle U.S. soldiers near Fort Philip Kearney. Published in Harper's Weekly, 1867.

eager to prove himself and advance his rank as an officer. Chief Red Cloud directed Crazy Horse, High Back Bone, and a group of other men to lure the cavalry farther from the fort. Crazy Horse and his band of warriors withdrew to a distant hillside and acted as decoys. Not surprisingly, Tasunke Witco acted independently and without fear. He dismounted. He lifted his horse's hoof and pretended to examine it, feigning that his horse had gone lame. He then took the horse's reins and led it about as though it were injured. The other warriors pretended to retreat, leaving Crazy Horse to fend for himself. Fetterman's force fell for the ruse. Tasunke Witco could see the enemy charging his way at full force! At the last moment, he mounted his pinto and rode off over the ridge, with Fetterman in pursuit.

Beyond, hidden in the folds of the landscape, waited at least 1,500 warriors! As the army descended the hilltop, the concealed warriors bolted from the snowy coulees in an overwhelming mass and surrounded the eighty-one soldiers. The Lakota warrior Fire Thunder, who was sixteen at the time, described what followed. "There were many bullets, but there were more arrows—so many that it was like a cloud of grasshoppers all above and around the soldiers; and our people, shooting across, hit each other. The soldiers were falling all the while they were fighting back up the hill, and their horses

The men in this photo offer a good example of the fierce Lakota warriors that fought Captain William Fetterman and his troopers.

got loose. Many of our people chased the horses, but I was not after horses; I was after Wasichus. When the soldiers got on top, there were not many of them left and they had no place to hide. They were fighting hard. We were told to crawl up on them, and we did. When we were close, someone yelled: 'Let us go! This is a good day to die. Think of the helpless ones at home!' Then we all cried, 'Hoka hey!' and rushed at them. I was young then and quick on my feet, and I was one of the first to get in among the soldiers. They got up and fought very hard until not one of them was alive."

At the last moment, Captain Fetterman and another officer, fearing they would be scalped alive, raised their pistols to their heads and committed suicide. Many Indians died, but most survived to celebrate a victory on the field of battle. Fetterman and all of his eighty men were killed. Among the Lakota, the fight became known as the Battle of the Hundred-in-the-Hand—because they had their hands filled with dead soldiers. News of the battle, the blood-splattered ground, and the severed heads and hands, stunned the American public. Newspapers called for revenge.

"Most of the Indians were mounted;
all were bedecked in their brightest colors,
their heads crowned with the brilliant war-bonnet,
their lances bearing the crimson pennant, bows strung,
and quivers full of barbed arrows."
—LIEUTENANT COLONEL GEORGE
ARMSTRONG CUSTER, *My Life on the Plains*

1867: The Summer Campaign

Public outcry put pressure on the U.S. government to take a stronger stand against the "Indian problem." The army sent a legion of soldiers west as part of the solution. Custer, now a lieutenant colonel in the 7th Cavalry Regiment, joined in what became known as the American Indian Wars. The summer campaign of 1867 against the Indians did not go well for the U.S. Army, or Custer.

Custer's cavalry tracked and chased the Indians across the plains. But the enemy refused to stand and fight like the Confederate Army had during the Civil War. Encounters resulted in brief skirmishes and ended with the Indians vanishing onto the prairies. Custer and his men grew frustrated with their tiresome pursuit after an enemy they could not pin down. Disillusioned soldiers began to desert. Many were lured away by the prospect of striking it rich in the gold fields of Montana and California. Custer felt he had to keep his men in line. He ordered his officers to shoot deserters. The grueling slog across the endless prairies began to wear on Armstrong, too. After months of aimlessly chasing Indians, Custer missed Libbie, whom he had not seen in all that time. He longed for her almost as much as he longed for war with the Indians. His personal passion overruled his duty as a commander: Custer abandoned his post of men and, with a small detachment of cavalry, he rode nonstop to be with Libbie in eastern Kansas. As a result, George Armstrong Custer was court-martialed for mistreating captured deserters and for being absent from his troops. He was removed from command and suspended from military duty for one year. Stunned by this humiliation, Lieutenant Colonel Custer thought his career as a soldier was finished.

The "Indian problem," however, continued. General Philip Sheridan, commander of the U.S. Army in the West, needed a fearless "Indian Fighter" to solve the problem. He needed someone exactly like Custer who would teach the Indians a lesson and force them to submit. George A. Custer was reinstated and told to crush the Indian resistance. Sheridan gave him orders "to destroy their villages and ponies; to kill or hang all warriors, and bring back all women and children."

There was another dynamic playing out in the country. Businessmen, along with government representatives, plotted to develop great swaths of land still inhabited by Indians. They planned to lay railways across the continent. They conducted their effort like a military operation using many of the management skills learned in the Civil War—how to mobilize thousands of men, feed them, keep them on task moving over forward. The new transportation system would be faster and more efficient than horse-drawn wagons, and it would connect the businesses in the East with those in the West. The influx of immigrants from Europe and Asia provided the labor force for the monumental undertaking— "the greatest engineering achievement of the nineteenth century." Working under deplorable conditions, they laid thousands of miles of rails. They also dug coal and iron ore from deep in the earth and forged steel in great mills that burned day and night. The steam-powered trains transported people, livestock, lumber, manufactured goods, and agricultural produce, creating an expanding trade network. Driven by gluttony, the ambitious businessmen created a new corporate economy. They were ruthless in their mistreatment of the workers and became absurdly rich in

Hunters shooting at a herd of bison from a train and along the tracks, 1871. Library of Congress.

the process. "But without them the transcontinental railroad would have remained a dream" on paper. This partnership of visionary businessmen and the muscle of the tireless workers developed countless new opportunities. Together they created the American Industrial Revolution and built a powerful new nation.

> "Either the progress of civilization must be stayed
> or the red man must be driven away or exterminated."
> —LIEUTENANT COLONEL
> GEORGE ARMSTRONG CUSTER

April 29, 1868: Treaty of Fort Laramie

Chief Red Cloud came to understand the futility of fighting the invading armies of the United States. Their overwhelming numbers and firepower made them unstoppable. In the end, his people would be destroyed. Along with some other chiefs, he compromised and put pen to paper. The treaty they signed promised to give to the Lakota people the Great Sioux Reservation. The enormous tract of land included all of the Black Hills. Red Cloud promised to settle his northern band of Oglala Lakota on the Great Sioux Reservation and directed his warriors to stop attacking settlements. In turn, the U.S. government agreed to remove three major forts along the Bozeman Trail. "On July 29, 1868, the troops at Fort C. F. Smith finally marched away. At dawn the next morning Crazy Horse and his warriors swept down on the post and set it afire. A few days later the soldiers left Forts Reno and Phil Kearny, which the Indians also burned." The signing of the treaty brought an end to Red Cloud's war. But other bands of Indians, under the leadership of Chief Sitting Bull and Crazy Horse, continued to resist. Crazy Horse despised the Indians who gave up the nomadic ways of the Lakota for handouts from the wasichus. He looked upon them as "loafers" or "Hang-Around-the-Forts." The ink was still drying on the treaty papers as army commanders planned attacks on the remaining Indian bands they viewed as "hostile."

> "The troops deployed into line at a gallop,
> and the Indian village rang with unearthly ...
> cries of infants and the wailing of women."
> —CAPTAIN ALBERT BARNITZ,
> 7th Cavalry at the Washita

November 27, 1868:
Battle of the Washita in Oklahoma

Lieutenant Colonel Custer had been publicly humiliated by his court-martial. He was determined to put a new shine on his reputation. If the Indian warriors would not stand and fight, he would attack their villages.

The Cheyenne chief, Black Kettle, was encamped on the banks of the Washita River. He had recently signed a peace agreement with the government. His band consisted of approximately 250 men, women, and children. Most had agreed to live peacefully with the wasichus. There were also many young Indian warriors in the camp who made a habit of riding off to attack wagon trains and settlements. In Custer's mind, they were all "savages." Armstrong would not fail in his new role as an Indian Fighter. He led his eight hundred mounted troopers on a forced night march across the snow-covered landscape. The blue light of the moon showed the way. Like a brilliant star, the planet Venus burned in the predawn. The Cheyenne called it the Morning Star. Cannons fired and Custer's horde of men rode into the valley, attacking the sleeping village. Kate Bighead was a child in the camp at the time and recalled, "It was early in the morning when the soldiers began the shooting. There had been a big storm, and there was snow on the ground. All of us jumped from our beds, and all of us started running to get away. I was barefooted, as were almost all the others. Our [tipis] and all of our property we had to leave behind were burned by the white men." Scores of people, as many as one hundred, were gunned down or put to

Called the Washita Massacre by the Lakota and the Battle of Washita by the U.S. government: At dawn Custer and his men attacked a sleeping village of Cheyenne on the Washita River in present-day Oklahoma, slaughtering women, men, and children.

the sword. Others fled, escaping into the woodland along the river. Black Kettle and his wife fell dead in the snow.

Afterward, all the winter food supplies and tipis were torched. Any survivors, who were in hiding, would be left to starve or freeze to death. Custer ordered all nine hundred Indian horses slaughtered so that there could be no escape. It was not an undertaking that the troopers enjoyed; they were horsemen, after all. And a horseman of any worth loves the beautiful animal. Blood soaked the frozen ground, turning white to red.

During the fight, one of Custer's officers, Major Joel Elliott, led nineteen men in pursuit of fleeing Cheyenne. The major and his men disappeared down the valley and did not return. Custer sent a detachment to find them. A gathering force of Indians from other villages turned them back. Custer assumed Major Elliott's entire command had perished. He felt it was too dangerous to remain in the valley of the Washita River; many Cheyenne warriors, from other camps, were converging on them. The Boy General lost twenty of his men in the fight, but he was triumphant! He took prisoners—fifty-three women and children. Back east, some people called the fight a massacre of innocent Indian people. The front pages of American newspapers praised it as a great and necessary victory. The Cheyenne would remember what Custer had done to them. They gave him a new name—Son of the Morning Star; the man who attacks before dawn.

Among the military ranks, many soldiers resented the fact that Custer had left Major Elliott and his men behind. They felt the honorable thing to do was to stay on the field of battle until all men were accounted for, dead or alive. One man in particular, Captain Frederick Benteen, seethed with anger. He believed the glory-seeking Custer had abandoned Elliott's men.

Major Joel Elliott and his men were found scalped and mutilated like the corpses of Lt. Kidder and his detachment pictured here and that had been killed one year earlier. The Indians called both incidents "fights." The American press called them "massacres."

Captain Frederick Benteen

In time, Benteen's resentment toward Custer would turn to hatred, with a final and tragic outcome. The bodies of Major Elliott and his men were eventually found where they had been surrounded, killed, and mutilated.

> "Crazy Horse would always jump off his horse to fire . . .
> He wanted to be sure that he hit what he aimed at."
> —HE DOG, OGLALA LAKOTA

1870: A Bad Place for a Fight

Crazy Horse and High Back Bone led a horse-stealing raid against the Shoshone. "It was in the fall," remembered He Dog. "There was a drizzly rain turning into snow." When their band came upon the Shoshone encampment, Crazy Horse resisted. He believed that they were outnumbered by the enemy. High Back Bone was itching for a fight; he insisted upon attacking. The lifelong friends agreed to disagree. The raid was on. The Shoshone responded immediately with a mounted counterattack. High Back Bone's horse was wounded and went down. The enemy pushed back the Lakota and killed High Back Bone. Crazy Horse and his men were forced to retreat. Crazy Horse felt he had no choice but to leave his friend—the same friend and teacher with whom he had learned to hunt as a youth. Together they had fought many battles, including the time they acted as decoys in the Fetterman Fight. Days later, Crazy Horse returned to retrieve the body of his best friend. Coyotes had beaten him to the fallen warrior. All that remained were shredded body parts.

"All Indians not on reservations are hostile
and will remain so until killed off."
—WILLIAM TECUMSEH SHERMAN

1874: Custer's Expedition
to the Black Hills

The conquest continued. Lieutenant Colonel Custer was ordered to lead an expedition of one thousand men into the heart of Lakota lands. He marched into the Black Hills. There he found forest-covered slopes with great stands of timber, flower-filled meadows with herds of elk and deer, and flowing mountain streams. Most important, he found gold! All of the Black Hills had been given to the Indians in the 1868 Treaty of Fort Laramie. Nevertheless, the words on the treaty paper could not keep gold prospectors out. News of the discovery of the yellow treasure spread like wildfire. Miners came by the tens of thousands—more miners than Lakota. Kate Bighead, now a young woman and living with her people in Black Hills country, remembered, "White people found gold there, so the Indians had to move out. The Cheyennes were told they must go to another reservation . . . It was no use, as the white people might want that reservation too."

In 1874, Custer wrote *My Life on the Plains*, describing his many adventures as an Indian Fighter for the U.S. Cavalry. He told readers that the Indian was "a *savage* in every sense of the word . . . one whose cruel and ferocious nature far exceeds that of any wild beast of the desert." The book became a best seller and rejuvenated his status as a national celebrity.

In his book, Custer criticized the military for not providing adequate supplies for soldiers on the frontier. He went further and accused the government Indian agencies who oversaw the reservations of not delivering rations to the Indians and instead were pocketing the proceeds for themselves. Further still, members of President Ulysses S. Grant's administration, including the president's own brother, were also skimming Indian agency funds for themselves. Custer's "finger pointing" at the corruption in Grant's administration infuriated the president. Custer also observed that the government was providing the Indians with rifles for hunting, but the rifles were also being used to attack wagon trains and to fight against the army.

In a surprise gesture, Custer wrote, "In studying the Indian character, while shocked and disgusted by many of his traits and customs, I find much to be admired." Armstrong simulated their dress, wearing fringed buckskins and a beaded knife sheath. Crazy Horse was a contradiction, too. Though he hated the arrogance and gluttony of the white man, he prized their horses and rifles. He often wore the white man's buttoned shirt. Custer made clear his final judgment on the Indian. "Civilization may and should do much for him, but it can never civilize him . . . Nature intended him for a savage state . . . He cannot be himself and be civilized."

Columns of cavalry, artillery, and wagons, commanded by Lieutenant Colonel George A. Custer, crossing the plains of Dakota Territory during the 1874 Black Hills expedition

> "My lodges were many, but now they are few.
> The White Man wants all."
> —RED CLOUD, OGLALA LAKOTA

Tasunke Witco's Revenge

Around this same time, Crazy Horse was shaken by a terrible event. He had been away from his wife and daughter on a horse-stealing raid against a Crow village. When he returned home he found that his four-year-old daughter had fallen ill with a fever and died. He was stricken with a sorrow that chokes a man's breath. For days he sat beneath the burial scaffold where his little one had been laid to rest. Tasunke Witco sobbed openly in mourning. The sun passed overhead by day and the stars turned overhead at night. He prayed to Wakan Tanka for answers, but none came. Slowly, his grief turned to rage. He blamed the loss of his child on the encroaching wasichus—they had brought nothing but disease and destruction. He would have revenge against those who were stealing his way of life! Like a lone wolf, he would fight for his people. Armed with his bow and arrows and a stout war club, he rode into his sacred Paha Sapa. There he randomly attacked and killed the intruders. He would ride into the camp of unsuspecting gold miners and in short order kill two or three men. Across Indian country other warriors joined in revenge killing to protect their lands and their way of life. An angry public called for military protection.

Crazy Horse sits beneath his daughter's burial scaffold.

> "The Indians' bones must enrich the soil,
> before the plough of civilized man can open it."
> —THOMAS FARNHAM

Spring 1876: The Indian Problem

Government officials were compelled to buy back the Black Hills. They forced the sale and called upon the tribes to abandon their treaty land and move onto a smaller reservation by January 31, 1876. Red Cloud's people and others moved, but Crazy Horse and his Oglala followers refused. The leader of the Hunkpapa band also refused the white man's orders. His name was Sitting Bull, and he commanded a large force of warriors. When these separate bands joined together, they numbered in the thousands. They intended to keep Paha Sapa and the vast prairies there about. The government labeled those who resisted "hostiles." The time had come for the government to finally end the "Indian problem."

Chief Sitting Bull, Tatanka Iyotake,
Hunkpapa Lakota

In the spring, the U.S. Army devised a massive attack to surround, subdue, and defeat the hostile Indians with a force of 3,100 cavalry, infantry, and Indian scouts. General George Crook would attack from the south with approximately 1,300 men, including 260 Crow and Shoshone scouts (enemies of the Lakota). Colonel John Gibbon would come from the west with approximately 400 men and more than 50 Crow scouts. General Alfred H. Terry would advance from the north with a column of 1,000 soldiers. He divided his column, sending a force from the east—the 7th Cavalry, under the command of Lieutenant Colonel

Left to right: General Alfred Terry, Colonel John Gibbon, and General George Crook

George Armstrong Custer. His regiment of 650 horsemen included 45 Crow and Arikara scouts. They rode "carrying the General's personal headquarters flag—a swallow-tailed guidon of red over blue with crossed swords, the same he had used during the Civil War."

Throughout his courtship and marriage to Libbie, Armstrong had frequently written letters to her and she to him. They loved each other with true fondness. Before his departure Custer put pen to paper. "My darling—I have but a few moments to write, as we move at twelve, and I have my hands full of preparations . . . Do not be anxious about me . . . I hope to have a good report to send you by the next mail."

> "The Wasichus made the treaty … that said [the land]
> would be ours as long as the grass should grow and water flow."
> —BLACK ELK, OGLALA LAKOTA

June 17, 1876: The Battle Where the Girl Saved Her Brother or the Battle of the Rosebud, Montana Territory

Tasunke Witco was never officially reinstated as a Shirt Wearer. None the less, because of his fearsome leadership his reputation was restored and again everyone viewed him as a Lakota chief. In early June, Chief Sitting Bull called for all Lakota, Cheyenne, and Arapaho tribes willing to resist to come together. Crazy Horse came with his large following of Oglala. Chief Gall arrived with his band of Hunkpapa, as did Two Moon with his Cheyenne band. Others came from the forts and agencies where they had spent the winter. Their village, to the west of Rosebud Creek, increased to an enormous size. Kate Bighead was there with her Cheyenne people. She recalled, "The grass grew high and our ponies became strong. Our men killed many buffalo, and we women tanned many skins and stored up much meat." They celebrated with the traditional Sun Dance, the Wiwanyang Wacipi, a ceremony in which men pierce their chests and tie themselves with cords to the sacred tree. They prayed to Father Sun, the source of all life on earth.

Everyone was in good spirits until Lakota scouts rode into camp with alarming news—a large force of bluecoats was advancing from the south. It was General Crook's column of more than 1,300 men. In Sitting Bull's camp, the warriors prepared to defend their people. They tied feathers in their hair, painted themselves and their horses. Although there wasn't a hierarchy of

Warriors tether themselves to the sacred tree during the Sun Dance ceremony, called the Wiwanyang Wacipi.

authority, Sitting Bull was the acknowledged head chief. He was an older man and had exhausted himself during the Sun Dance. He remained behind, offering prayers for success. Sitting Bull urged the men forward, "Steady men! Remember how to hold a gun! Brace up now! Brace up!" He appointed Tasunke Witco to lead the fight.

Crazy Horse, his shoulders painted with hailstones and his cheek emblazoned with a lightning bolt, rode forward into battle like a fierce wolf. In his hair he wore the feather of a red-tailed hawk. He was followed close behind by more than a thousand howling warriors. The bloody fight that followed lasted all day. Dozens fell on both sides. Crazy Horse led several fierce charges through the soldier's ranks. He Dog remembered, "When he came on the field of battle he made everybody brave." Crook's Shoshone and Crow allies fought brilliantly and prevented what could have ended in slaughter for the bluecoats. Nonetheless, General Crook's force suffered a defeat in what became known as the Battle of the Rosebud. He had orders to press the Indians from the south; instead he withdrew his army. He would not advance northward into the valley of the Little Bighorn. The Lakota called the fight the Battle Where the Girl Saved Her Brother, because a young Cheyenne woman rode with the men. When her brother's horse was shot down, she raced in to rescue him. Soldiers were shooting at her from two sides, but she still managed to save him.

> "The largest Indian camp on the North American
> continent is ahead and I am going to attack it."
> —LIEUTENANT COLONEL GEORGE ARMSTRONG CUSTER

June 25–26, 1876: The Battle of
the Little Bighorn, Montana Territory

The Lakota and their allies left the valley of Rosebud Creek. Their force had grown in size as more Indians left the reservations and joined them. Now their horse herd numbered more than 12,000, all in need of fresh pasturage and water. They found a comfortable setting near the Greasy Grass River. The white men called it the Little Bighorn. The different bands had become a huge village. "All told there were as many as 8,000 to 10,000 Indians, with between 1,500 and 2,000 fighting men—many of them young men from the agencies, fed and armed, ironically, by the U.S. government." Kate Bighead said, "There were more Indians . . . than I ever saw together anywhere else." Late into the night they celebrated their victory with bonfires and singing and dancing. Of course, Crazy Horse did not participate. Others danced about roaring fires dressed in wolf and deer skins, with eagle feathers tied in their hair. Tasunke Witco stood alone in the shadows, considering what would come next.

Custer knew he was close on the trail of the hostiles. He pushed his men and their horses hard. They rode day and night, resting little. An overconfident Custer did not want his men to be slowed by any unnecessary weight. They brought no cannons or rotary-fire Gatling guns. The 7th Cavalry left behind their sabers—not needed. Custer believed rifles and pistols would win the day.

Advancing from the east, Custer expected Generals Crook and Terry and Colonel Gibbon to be approaching from opposing sides in a massive surrounding action. His force would be the spearhead that entrapped the hostiles. He planned to surprise the Indians, crush them, and declare a great victory that would be hailed in the newspapers back home. Not all the men in Custer's command were eager to engage the Indians. Two officers, Captain Frederick Benteen and Major Marcus Reno, disliked the Boy General. In particular, since the Battle of the Washita, Captain Benteen had grown to despise him for his arrogance and for placing his personal glory before the welfare of his men. Reno was not a clear thinker, often under the influence of alcohol.

Armstrong had intended to rest his exhausted men and horses for one day before his final assault. He would attack on June 26. But, in the predawn light of June 25, his Crow scouts reported that they could see the Lakota village in the far distance. In disbelief, they told Custer that it was the biggest camp of Lakota they had ever seen. They suggested the Lakota might pack their belongings and try to flee. The lieutenant colonel bristled; he would not allow the Indians to escape. Not this time. The Crow scouts warned that there were more Indians in the valley than the 7th Cavalry had bullets.

Major Marcus Reno

Ashishishe, known as Curly, Crow Tribe,
was a scout for Custer, circa 1885.

Lieutenant Colonel Custer divided his force into three attack groups as they advanced into the valley of the Little Bighorn. Major Reno and his 150 mounted troopers were to charge downstream along the river bottom toward the village. Captain Benteen, with 130 horsemen, was to advance down the valley on the left and fight any Indians they encountered. A fourth troop would bring up the rear with civilian packers, who guided 175 pack mules carrying rations and ammunition. Custer and his 225 men would advance on the high bluffs to the right of the river. A Crow scout named Half Yellow Face protested. "Do not divide your men. There are too many of the enemy for us." Custer dismissed the comment. "You do the scouting, and I will attend to the fighting."

Horses wading in water next to a tipi encampment on the Little Bighorn River

Chief Gall, Phizí, Hunkpapa Lakota leader, in 1881

Kate Bighead recounted how she and a friend began the morning. "We found our women friends bathing in the river, and we joined them. Other groups, men, women and children, were playing in the water at many places along the stream. Some boys were fishing. All of us were having a good time. It was somewhere past the middle of the forenoon. Nobody was thinking of any battle coming."

Crazy Horse sat in the dappled shade of cottonwood trees enjoying a midday meal prepared by Black Shawl. He was pleased by the recent success on Rosebud Creek and felt a strong sense of unity among his people. On the nearby hills, women were digging for prairie turnips. In the cool waters of the Greasy Grass, children splashed and boys watered their horses. A commotion arose in the distance; a mixture of gunfire and people shouting, "Soldiers are coming! They are charging!" Bullets ripped through the air like angry wasps clipping leaves from the trees above. Tasunke Witco stepped into his tipi. The Lakota warrior prepared himself with sacred medicine. He quickly tied a hawk feather in his hair and painted himself with hailstones and a thunderbolt. Grabbing his weapons, he mounted up.

Major Reno had started his day with liquor. He was already drunk when he led his 150 troopers and 35 Arikara scouts at a gallop. One of the cavalrymen, Private William O. Taylor, recalled that Major Reno commanded, "Charrrrge!" and as Taylor "looked back Major Reno was just taking a bottle from his lips." Overhead, the sun seared its white circle in the cloudless blue. Reno's charging cavalry stirred a thundering dust cloud as they approached the outermost part of the village. The Arikara scouts were happy to join in the fight against their blood enemies. Chief Gall responded—hundreds of his Hunkpapa Lakota warriors counterattacked in a fury. They repelled the bluecoats with a wall of bullets and arcing arrows. Several troopers fell. Private Taylor described the "increasing number of Indian warriors coming toward us as fast as their ponies could travel, a whooping, howling mass of the best horsemen, the most cruel and fiercest fighters in all our country." Major Reno's assault faltered. He ordered his men to halt, dismount, and use their single-shot carbine rifles from a standing position. "Arrows whistled past and smashed into trees; bullets zipped by, raining twigs and branches down onto the men." Reno was

William O. Taylor

trying to communicate with one of his Indian scouts standing nearby, named Bloody Knife. "One round hit Bloody Knife in the back of the head . . . his blood and brains spattered Reno's face and front." Reno "wiped bits of bone and blood off his face." The fearsome attack of the Lakota put him in a panic. The addled man was unaccustomed to the sight of blood. Reno ordered his men to remount and retreat.

They fled into the woods and crossed the Little Bighorn at the base of the eastern bluffs. Taylor recounted his escape. "After a hard struggle I climbed the steep bank, the rapid pace and exertion over the river had completely exhausted my horse and he stood trembling with fatigue and refused to go any further . . . I dismounted and amid whistling of bullets stood there for a few moments." With swarming Indians in hot pursuit, he had no choice but to abandon his broken-winded horse. He paired up with another trooper named Myers and they continued the climb on foot. "We walked along quite close together for a few feet when with but the single exclamation of 'Oh,' Myers pitched forward face down to the ground. I bent over him but he was dead, shot between the left ear and eye." Taylor struggled onward alone, finally reaching the high ground, where he joined Reno and the desperate survivors. Together they formed a defensive stand—a redoubt.

In the hills to the southwest, Captain Benteen wandered over broken terrain and made no contact with Indians. Instead of following Custer's orders to fight, Benteen dawdled. He resented taking orders from the younger and higher-ranking officer. Within the army there had always existed personal rivalries that pitted some officers against each other. On this day, such long-held resentments would contribute to Custer's undoing.

Custer and his immediate command rode along the high bluffs on the east side of the Little Bighorn River. For the first time, he grasped the enormity of the situation. Below and extending for more than two miles lay the largest gathering of Indians he had ever laid eyes on. The lieutenant colonel was not a man known to retreat. He shouted to his men, "We've caught them napping. We've got them!" He sent a messenger to Captain Benteen with the orders "Ride as fast as you can, and tell him to hurry. Tell him it's a big village, and I want him to be quick, and to bring the ammunition packs."

Crazy Horse rode directly toward the sound of the fighting, gathering fellow warriors as he went. Cries went up from the villagers. "Crazy Horse is coming! Crazy Horse is coming!" He called out, "Ho-ka hey! It is a good day to fight! It is a good day to die! Strong hearts, brave hearts, to the front!" He gathered a force of mounted men, who joined Chief Gall and the Hunkpapa Lakotas. Together they forced a complete retreat of Major Reno's command on the south side of the village. Many bluecoats fell and were scalped. Those who managed to escape crossed the river and dug in on a hilltop.

Kate Bighead described the chaotic scene. "Throngs of [Indian] men on horses were racing toward . . . where the guns were clattering . . . there was great excitement. Old men were helping the young warriors in dressing and painting themselves for battle. Some women were bringing war horses from the herds. Other women were . . . running away with only their children or with small packs in hands. I saw one [Lakota] woman just staying at one spot, jumping up and down and screaming, because she could not find her little son."

Crazy Horse turned his attention from the troopers pinned down on the ridge to Custer's attacking force on the east side of the river. He rode back to the northern end of the village. As he rode, he blew his bone whistle with the shrill cry of a soaring hawk. He rallied hundreds of mounted warriors as he went. Women offered support with the trilling call. Short Bull remembered hearing Crazy Horse say, "There's a good fight coming over the hill. That's where the big fight is going to be." Crazy Horse laughed. "He made a joke of it." Tasunke Witco and 1,000 mounted warriors crossed the Greasy Grass in a maneuver to block Custer's advance of 200-odd men.

Captain Benteen received Custer's orders to advance, bring more ammunition, and reinforce his men. Instead, the grudgeful Benteen joined forces with Reno in a "holding" position on the hilltop. All they could, or would, do is hunker down and hope Custer's men could defend themselves.

The midday sun burned overhead with the sweltering heat of an open-door oven. Unknown to Custer, Reno and Benteen were still miles away to the south. They were surrounded and under vicious attack. Custer continued to press his command and their horses northward along the high bluffs. To his left, across the river, he could see the heart of the village. Here, he made yet another grave mistake. He split his force again, sending two companies of mounted men down the riverbank with orders to cross the river and strike the middle of the village. But there were too many Indians. The two companies were repulsed and compelled to rejoin Custer. The steep uphill climb exhausted both horses and men. In the meantime, Custer continued northward with his remaining force. All the while, hundreds of warriors emerged from the river bottom and attacked his left flank and rear guard. They killed scores of bluecoats.

Armstrong pushed on. He still planned to reach the northern end of the village and stop the escape of any cowardly Indians. To his utter dismay, Crazy Horse met him and the 7th Cavalry head-on. Tasunke Witco had amassed his swarm of mounted warriors at precisely the right moment.

Overwhelmed by the frontal assault, Custer had no choice but to halt his attack. Amid the melee of yelling men and their terrified animals, the lieutenant colonel rallied his men to a position on high ground. The sweat-lathered horses trembled with utter fatigue as they stumbled uphill. Sitting Bull said, "They were brave men, but they were too tired . . . When they got off from their horses they could not stand firmly on their feet. They swayed to and fro—so my young men have told me—like the limbs of cypresses in a great wind."

No one in Custer's immediate command survived to tell what happened next. But historians, archaeologists, and the surviving Indians suggest the following: From the high ground, Custer looked back. He was alone with only eighty-odd men. In desperation he must have thought, "Where in God's name are Reno and Benteen?" They were supposed to provide reinforcement. Custer and his remaining command were surrounded and being overrun by a horde of yelling, painted warriors. Bullets split the air above. Metal-tipped arrows were falling everywhere. The projectiles killed soldiers, horses, and unfortunate Indians caught in the crossfire. The young Lakota Iron Hawk later said, "I met a soldier on horseback, and I let him have it. The arrow went through from side to side under his ribs and it stuck out on both sides."

The bluecoats could not shoot and reload their single-shot rifles quickly enough. One trooper galloped away across the prairie, hoping to escape. He was pursued by several yelping Indians. Exhaustion quickly caught up with the fleeing bluecoat. He pulled up his mount, put his pistol to his head, and pulled the trigger. Other soldiers had also saved one last bullet for themselves in the event of capture and used them this day. They feared being cut up and scalped alive.

Kate Bighead crossed the river on horseback and watched from a distance as men collapsed in their death struggle. She said, "The Indians were using bows and arrows more than they were using guns . . . a rain of arrows . . . hit many soldiers and their horses by falling and sticking into their heads or their backs." The tumult of battle stirred a choking cloud of dust and gunsmoke that smudged out the sun. Shadowy figures of men fought with fury, to the death. Two Moon said, "The shooting was quick, quick. Pop-pop-pop very fast. Some of the soldiers were down on their knees, some standing. The smoke was like a great cloud, and everywhere the [Lakota] went the dust rose like smoke. We circled all around them—swirling like water round a stone. We shoot, we ride fast, we shoot again. Soldiers drop, and horses fall on them. Soldiers in line drop, but one man rides up and down the line, all the time shouting . . . I don't know who he was. He was a brave man." The withering staccato of gunfire and the screams of men and of horses merged into a roaring storm. An Arapaho recalled, "Crazy Horse . . .

was the bravest man I ever saw. He rode closest to the soldiers, yelling to his warriors. All the soldiers were shooting at him, but he was never hit." Tasunke Witco dismounted and fought his way through the clamorous haze on foot. The painted thunderbolt and hailstones emblazoned on his body gave him courage. The hawk feather in his hair guided every movement. Over his head he swung a skull-crushing war club with which he unleashed a lifetime of pent-up rage. His followers joined in the killing. Kate Bighead saw how some of the horror-stricken bluecoats died in the turmoil. She said, "I saw them go at shooting each

Chief Two Moon, Ishaynishus, Cheyenne

Following pages: The Battle of the Little Bighorn; called the Greasy Grass Fight by the Lakota

other and shooting themselves." Iron Hawk would later say, "These Wasichus wanted it, and they came to get it, and we gave it to them."

Above the din and still mounted, Armstrong shouted orders to his men. Immediately the remaining bluecoats responded. They reined their horses into a circle, head to tail, and shot them dead. The circle of fallen animals formed a barricade. The desperate soldiers tried to take cover behind the breastworks, but the hailstorm of bullets and arrows was too much.

The trooper next to Armstrong took a bullet and pitched forward with a moan. A bullet slammed into Custer's ribs. He faltered but stood against the pain. He fumbled with his pistol, trying to reload. He shoved one last bullet into the chamber . . . No time to consider the mistakes he had made this day. No time for one last prayer to the god of Manifest Destiny. The end had come.

On the morning of June 27, General Alfred Terry and Colonel John Gibbon arrived from the north with more than 800 soldiers. They found what remained of Custer's fallen command. The bold Indian Fighter and 262 of his men lay dead. The besieged Reno and Benteen warily emerged from their hilltop redoubt five miles away. Private Taylor, along with the other survivors, greeted their rescuers "with prolonged cheers." Sitting Bull and Crazy Horse had fled, leading their people in different directions. They set fire to the dry prairie grass behind them so that they could not be followed and hunted down. Custer and all his men had been stripped naked and their bodies mutilated. All their weapons and clothing had been taken by the victors. Custer had two bullet wounds. There was one in his chest and one in his left temple.

No one knows how many Indians died defending their village. News of the terrible battle was telegraphed back East. When word of the "massacre" reached Libbie, she collapsed in grief. Her golden-haired Boy General was dead. At first, Americans refused to accept the unbelievable. Then reality set in. The Indians had defeated the United States Army in a great battle on the western frontier at a place called the Little Bighorn. The public demanded an immediate response— the final conquest and surrender of the Indians on the Great Plains.